MOUNTAIN

MOUNTAIN BIKE
MAINTENANCE AND REPAIR

Thomas Roegner

CYCLE PUBLISHING
San Francisco

Copyright © 2003, Cycle Publishing, for the English-language edition
Copyright © 2002, Delius Klasing Verlag, for the German edition

Printed in Hong Kong

Publisher's Information:
Cycle Publishing (formerly Van der Plas Publications)
1282 7th Avenue
San Francisco, CA 94122
USA

Tel.: (415) 665-8214
Toll-free tel. (U.S. and Canada only): 1-877-353-1207
Fax: (415) 753-8572
Web site: http://www.cyclepublishing.com
E-mail: pubrel@cyclepublishing.com

Distributed or represented to the book trade by:
USA: Midpoint Trade Books, Kansas City, KS
UK: Chris Lloyd Sales and Marketing / Orca Book Services, Poole, Dorset
Canda: New Society Publishing, Gabriola Island, BC
Australia: Tower Books, Frenchs Forest, NSW

Cover design:
Kent Lytle, Lytle Design, Alameda, CA

Publisher's Cataloging in Publication Data
Roegner, Thomas, Mountain Bike Maintenance and Repair: Your Complete Guide to Keeping Your Mountain
Bike Going Strongly. Translated and adapted for the English-language market by Rob van der Plas
P. 24.0 cm. Includes index
1. Bicycles and bicycling—handbooks and manuals
I. Title
II. Authorship
Library of Congress Control Number: 2003105928
ISBN 1-892495-37-6 (softcover edition); ISBN 1-892495-87-2 (electronic edition)

TABLE OF CONTENTS

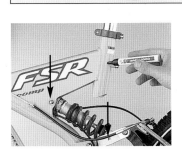

KNOW YOUR BIKE,
USE YOUR BIKE

Compared to the overall history of the bicycle, which goes back to the year 1817, the mountain bike is just a pretty young thing—barely 20 years old at the time of writing. However, no other type of bicycle has seen anything like the spectacular developments in design, materials, and equipment that's been so crucial in the short history of the mountain bike.

First developed in California as little more than an upgraded clunker bicycle for descending steep hills, today's mountain bike is a far cry from what the pioneers were riding. Within a brief span of years, superbly effective brake systems, smoothly shifting gear trains, and sophisticated suspensions add safety and comfort to the once-humble mountain bike. After initial reluctance, the bicycle industry has embraced the mountain bike and its development—after all, this is the bike that "rescued" the industry from what would otherwise have become a protracted slump in the 1980s and 1990s.

But part of the mountain bike's success lies not with its technology but with it's effect on the rider. Like no other type of bicycle before it, this has become a "bike for all seasons," as suitable for a quick trip to the store as it is for a race up and down the nearest slope, as good for a two-week bike tour as it is for the commute to work or college, and as much fun in fall or winter as it is by fine weather. In short, the mountain bike is the ideal vehicle to positively effect your way of life and the way you look at the world.

Whether alone, with friends, in a casual group, or an organized one, the experience of your interaction with the machine and the natural environment are highly invigorating on the mountain bike—much more so than in any other sport. This also helps explain the phenomenal success of organized mountain biking tours and the spectacular popularity of very challenging rides, be they crossing Alaska in winter or the Alps in summer.

The experience of being able to cover 50 miles or more while conquering cumulative ascents in excess of 10,000 ft, day after day, gives you a new look at your abilities and the forces of nature. The experience is something that can make you an "addict" to such tours—and it's by no means a bad addiction. Once you've been bitten by the mountain bike bug, you'll probably want to continue your quest for higher, faster, steeper, rougher, and more.

UNDERSTANDING YOUR BIKE

Despite all those extremes, the mountain bike has remained relatively simple as compared to other types of equipment for everyday use. Whereas you'll hesitate taking computers, video equipment, etc. apart to try and fix them yourself, you'll have the comfort of knowing that maintaining and fixing your mountain bike is

assembly of common parts that can each be adjusted, disassembled, and reassembled by the rider him- or herself. And once you know how those components interact, you've mastered the art of mountain bike maintenance reasonably well. Sure, there will be some things for which you have to consult a bike shop, and certain ones that require tools and knowledge only available there. But even in those cases, being an informed customer will be of great help in getting the problem fixed quickly—if only because you don't come in saying "there's something wrong with my bike," but will be able to accurately pinpoint the source and the nature of the problem.

And out on the trail, you never have to be helpless. Once you know what (if anything) is most

The mountain bike dissected. Once you understand the way each of its parts work, you'll be well prepared to take good care of your bike.

something you can handle. With a bit of knowledge—what this book imparts—you'll rarely find yourself in the situation of wondering what's wrong and what to do about it.

Even a "hi-tech" mountain bike—despite all the titanium, carbon fiber, and what have you—is still a relatively simple

likely to go wrong, you'll know what to carry in the way of tools, you'll know what to do about specific problems, and how to get yourself home even if it's with only a provisional fix. Oh yes, sometimes things really break, and we can't help you with that, but at least you'll know what you can do and what you can't.

THE JOYS OF SELF-HELP

This book will show you how to maintain and repair your mountain bike. It will show you what kind of tools you need and how to use them. Above all, it will help you maintain your bike in a state of "good health." Preventive maintenance, the subject of a large part of this book, is the key to riding without breakdowns, and will even help you prevent injury to yourself.

Mountain biking adventure. There's no better way to experience nature than by riding your mountain bike. You can cover significant distances out in the wilds. When properly maintained, following the advice in this book, the bike won't let you down.

Your investment in learning to understand the bike and its parts, their maintenance, and repair will pay off handsomely in an increased appreciation of the machine and the sport. The feeling of knowing how to do all this yourself, of not being dependent on someone else, should be an important aspect of a sport that puts the rider in charge.

The material included in this book was carefully selected by the author, in cooperation with the technical editor and the test edi-

tor of a major mountain biking magazine, on the basis of what are the most frequently needed operations and the most frequently asked questions of real-life mountain bikers.

In addition to "straightforward" maintenance and repair tips, we've included extensive instructions on how to tune such mechanisms as suspension systems, brakes, and derailleur gears. Finally, we've included advice for selecting a bike in the first place

and choosing "upgrade" components in line with your personal needs. All this together should help you get the most out of your mountain bike.

2 SELECTING YOUR MOUNTAIN BIKE

There's a lot to choose from: hardtails with and without front suspension, and full suspension bikes; steel, aluminum, titanium, and composite frames; different kinds of brakes, different types of suspension, and so on. Which model you choose depends on the terrain and what kind of rider you are. Here's some advice on helping you make your choice.

Unlike the old cruiser or three-speed, a mountain bike is not just any old piece of equipment. In fact, it has become both a cult object for bikies and at the same time an engineering challenge for the bike industry. Consequently, the mountain bikes themselves have become more complicated, while the market for them has become more complex—it has become quite hard to tell what's the difference between various makes and models, and just as hard to tell what they may have in common. On a more positive note, that does mean that there are so many variations that there will be at least one bike that offers exactly what corresponds to your needs, however "picky" you may be.

In this chapter, you'll learn about the various available models and their components, highlighting both their advantages and disadvantages with respect to different types of riders, riding styles, and terrain types. In particular, we'll distinguish between the traditional unsuspended mountain bike, the so-called hardtail (i.e. one with only front suspension, and an unsprung rear wheel), and the full-suspension bike.

Whereas in the olden days the major issue was whether a frame was made of aluminum or steel, today the argument is largely between adherents of the hardtail and the full-suspension bike. It's a decision with which anyone planning to buy a new mountain bike will be confronted. Even those who buy a "bare" frame on which to install the various components themselves have to decide one way or another, because the full-suspension bike requires a specific frame with built-in rear suspension.

Essentially, the question about the "best" mountain bike type for your use can be determined on the basis of your own objectives. If you do most of your riding under real off-road conditions with steep downhill sections and rough terrain, especially if you do so at least twice a week, then the right type of bike for you is almost bound to be a full-suspension bike. If, on the other hand most of your riding is in less demanding terrain or if you don't ride frequently enough to justify the extra expense, then the "hardtail" will probably suit your needs better. Another argument in favor of the hardtail may be that you want to go touring, covering longer distances, for which you will want to minimize the weight and get a bike on which luggage can be carried, both of which are easier on a hardtail.

FRONT SUSPENSION

Early mountain bikes did not have suspension, neither front nor rear. "So why has suspension suddenly become so important?" you may ask. You may as well ask why today's cars have fuel injection and power windows, whereas the early cars did fine without those "gadgets." It's simply a matter of refinements that have become available as the product was further developed.

When the mountain bike was first developed, in the late 1970s and early 1980s, there simply were no suspension forks available

that could be installed on the mountain bike, and the riders depended entirely on the pressure in their tires to keep the bike on the ground without jolting the rider out of the saddle. It is well known from motorcycle racing, and was soon confirmed in mountain bike racing, that you could go faster, while controlling the bike better, if you could absorb the shocks from the terrain. So in the late 1980s, a couple of enterprising tinkerers and engineers independently developed various suspension forks. After that, enterprising companies soon took up production, and before long their advan-

THE UNIFIED REAR TRIANGLE

Just like the single-pivot swing arm, the unified rear triangle suspension has only a single, large pivot points at which the rear triangle is attached to the frame. The difference is the following: In the case of the unified rear triangle suspension, the crankset is part of the unified rear triangle that is suspended, whereas in the case of the single pivot swing arm, it is part of the front end, which is stationary. Consequently, the chain length is not affected by the suspension in any way.

However, there are some disadvantages too:

1. The suspension does not work as well when the rider is standing on the pedals as it does when seated.

2. As a result of the downward pressure on the pedals, an additional moment arm is created, which pushes down on the swing arm. If the unit is adjusted for soft response, the result is the so-called "jackknife effects" when riding uphill. That can only be prevented by selecting a pivot point for the rear triangle that lies relatively high above the bottom bracket, which is referred to as the "sweet spots" design. However, in that case, the suspension hardly works at all while standing on the pedals.

3. Depending on the design details, the distance between the seat and the bottom bracket changes more or less. The result of that is that the pedaling motion feels less smooth than it should be.

All these points add up to enough disadvantages to conclude that the unified rear triangle is on its way out, and fied rear triangle is on its way out, and

will be found only on older full-suspension bikes (anything built before 2002) and on cheaper machines.

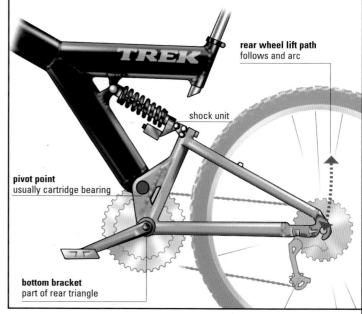

rear wheel lift path
follows and arc

shock unit

pivot point
usually cartridge bearing

bottom bracket
part of rear triangle

On account of its design, the disadvantages of the unified rear triangle—such as the jackknife effect and the stiffening of the suspension under some conditions—this design is on its way out. If you are only looking for comfort, and usually remain seated, this system is by no means inferior. However, for more ambitious or aggressive off-road cyclists, the unified rear triangle does not work as well as the designs with multiple pivots, i.e. 4-bar linkage and the parallelogram designs, which both work well, regardless of whether you are standing or sitting, and whether you're climbing or descending.

tages became so generally appreciated that every discerning bike manufacturer incorporated them on their bikes—and hardly a serious off-road rider wanted to do without them.

Whereas the early suspension forks were prone to all sort of problems, largely due to the penetration of dirt at the seals, their design has meanwhile evolved to the point where they are as reliable as any other part of the bike. At the same time, they have become lighter and easier to adjust.

The major difference between various suspension forks is a matter of "travel"—the dimension for the difference between the fully compressed and the unloaded condition. For weekend riders traveling in modest terrain, models with 40 to 60 mm travel (1.6 to 2.2 in.) are usually adequate. The most satisfactory models available today are those incorporating either coil springs or compressed air cartridges, combined with hydraulic damping. Elastomer-damped forks (using foam pads of different densities) are simple, cheap, and quite reliable; but they are not as compliant and responsive as coil-spring-based models—the former are intended only for casual riding.

This may be a good time to explain the difference between suspension and damping. Suspension without damping is perhaps best described as "springiness" or even "bounciness." As an impact from the road is absorbed by the spring, it stores the energy, which is released again, jolting the bike back up in the air, and back down, and up, etc.. The function of damping is to slow down this movement so that the initial impact is not taken quite so abruptly and the response will be a slower return to the original position, without bouncing up and down many times.

Buying a satisfactory suspension fork individually will set you back at least $200 (£120), although they can be included in a complete bike for significantly less money due to the bike manufacturers' ability to purchase at the very substantial OEM (Original Equipment Manufacturer's) discounts. If you have to buy one, e.g. as a replacement, watch for the ads in the major mountain

Many fast mountain bike riders still prefer the so-called "hardtail," i.e. a bike without rear suspension. These bikes are lighter and the rider's pedaling force is transferred more directly to the rear wheel.

biking publications offering previous years' models at substantial savings. See chapter 7 for extensive information on the installation of suspension forks, both on a bike that was originally designed for one and for bikes that were previously equipped with a rigid front fork.

As you move on to more challenging terrain and higher downhill speeds, you will want to choose more sophisticated forks with longer travel—all the way up to about 100 mm (4 in.), which is just about the maximum for use on hardtail bikes. That's because the modern hardtail is really nothing but the logical descendant of the early unsuspended mountain bikes. To take more travel, you need a radically redesigned frame, as offered mainly on full-suspension bikes. In full-suspension bikes, it seems the sky is the limit, both in the front and the rear, with travel all the way up to 200 mm (8 in.).

The price and the performance of a hardtail are primarily determined by the quality of the frame

SINGLE-PIVOT	FOUR BAR LINKAGE	UNIFIED REAR TRIANGLE
Advantages		
low weight	sensitive characteristics	favorable price (low manufacturing cost)
few pivot points	wide range of applications	low weight, low maintenance
not affected by pedaling	not affected by pedaling motion	totally active system (rear triangle suspended whether standing or seated)
Disadvantages		
poor response while standing	multiple pivots, high weight	no brake force compensation
distance between seat and bottom bracket varies	subject to wear	hard to carry
suspension ineffective while climbing	maintenance-intensive	difficult cable routing and front derailleur installation
Representative models		
Trek Y-models Fisher Joshua, K2	GT LTS, AMP, Specialized	Cannondale, Scott

THE SINGLE PIVOT SWINGARM

In the case of the single swingarm, the chainstays are pivoted at a point behind, and usually above, the bottom bracket, around which the rear triangle rotates. In the case of modern single-pivot full-suspension bikes, the pivot point is located about as high as the top of the middle chainring. The rear wheel axle of a single-pivot bike follows the contour of a circle segment when the suspension is activated.

On a typical single-pivot suspension bike, such as e.g. the Cannondale Super V, the main frame does not look like the conventional diamond shape but is in the form of a letter Y. A special case is formed by bikes such as the Rocky Mountain Element: Although these bikes are equipped with a large number of individual pivots, they are effectively still single-pivot models. This is because they are not equipped with the so-called Horst-link, which is a short linkage just in front of the dropouts on the chain stays. Consequently, on these bikes, rotation is around a single defined pivot point on the frame. All other linkage arrangements on these bikes do not serve to affect the movement of the wheel, but to facilitate movement of the suspension unit. For this reason, these bikes are also referred to as single-pivot systems with multiple linkages.

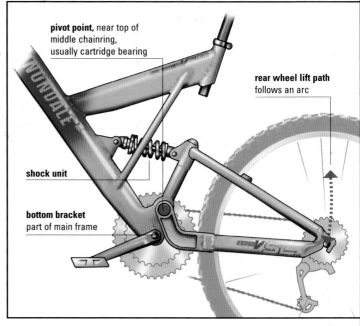

pivot point, near top of middle chainring, usually cartridge bearing

rear wheel lift path follows an arc

shock unit

bottom bracket part of main frame

Single-pivot systems are relatively popular. If they are well constructed, they usually have a large, well sealed industrial ball bearing unit, which makes them less wear- and maintenance-intensive. This type of frame is relatively cheap to produce for the manufacturer, which also results in a more modest price of the bicycle in the shop. Although single-pivot suspension bikes are not quite as versatile as four-bar suspension units, it can be stated that in today's market, they offer the best compromise between rigidity, low weight, ease of maintenance, and low price.

and of the components and the frame geometry. Unless you're really hard up, we recommend buying at least a hardtail, rather than buying a bike with a rigid fork. The increase in safety, speed, control, and comfort with a suspension fork is quite significant, and sooner or later you're bound to want to "move up" to the performance level offered by a suspension fork. That's when you'll discover that retrofitting a regular bike with a suspension fork is much less satisfactory and considerably more expensive than it would have been to purchase a bike with suspension fork right away.

One of the frame types that has recently made a comeback is the "cruiser" frame, familiar from the old American newsboy-style bike with curved frame tubes. This was the frame type on which the early, experimental, mountain bikes were based. Very few of these models have anything to recommend them other than their "cool" retro-look. They're cute city bikes but not really mountain bikes as such. You're almost certainly better served by a (lighter) conventional mountain bike frame if you're looking for a bike to ride off-road.

HARDTAIL VERSUS FULL-SUSPENSION BIKE

Although full-suspension bikes really come into their own on steep descents, it's no longer fair

Modern single-pivot suspension bikes are fun to ride uphill as well as down. These bikes are relatively easy to maintain because there is only one (usually rugged) bearing to worry about.

THE FOUR-BAR LINKAGE

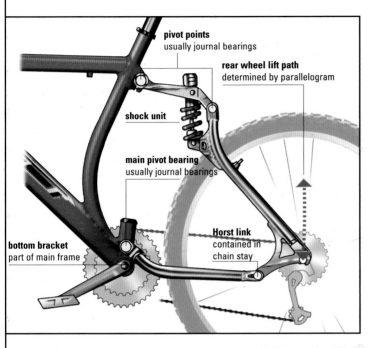

pivot points
usually journal bearings

rear wheel lift path
determined by parallelogram

shock unit

main pivot bearing
usually journal bearings

bottom bracket
part of main frame

Horst link
contained in
chain stay

In the case of the four-bar linkage, the rear of the frame is pivoted at four points and is equipped with a so-called Horst-link. This keeps the rear wheel going straight up and down, rather than following a circular path. It follows a geometric path that can be defined by the specific location and dimensions of the linkage, which makes the rear triangle work as a parallelogram. Consequently, the rear wheel goes almost straight up and down in response to jolts while riding over obstacles.

This principle is known by the acronym VPP, or Virtual Pivot Point. From the rider's standpoint, the advantage of this system is that the rider's pedaling motion does not affect the suspension in whichever gear is engaged. You will experience neither kick-back from the suspension on the pedals, nor reduced suspension effects when accelerating, standing on the pedals, nor when braking. In addition, this system is very responsive—providing you keep it well maintained and adjusted.

Four-bar linkages, such as those used, for example on the GT LTS or the Specialized Ground Control FSR bikes, are the most responsive of all types of rear suspension systems when it comes to eliminating power-consuming motion from influencing the drive train. However, the main problem of this design lies in the large number of relatively small pivots. Simple solutions, such as the journal bearings used in many of the linkage connections, wear out quickly and are consequently very maintenance-intensive. Four-bar linkage systems with industrial cartridge bearings, which require little maintenance, on the other hands, are often relatively heavy.

to characterize them merely as downhill bikes. Many modern full-suspension bikes offer a lot more comfort without sacrificing significantly in terms of weight and bike handling. Yes, usually the rear suspension "eats" some of your power output, which is especially noticeable when going uphill. However, on many fully-suspended bikes there is a method of partially or wholly locking out the rear suspension, so the drive is as direct as it is on any other bike.

Even in terms of weight, a lot has been achieved in recent years. Today, many full-suspension bikes weigh no more than 12 kg (26 lbs), a figure that was good for a rigid bike as recently as 1995. Since the suspension spares the

rider's body some of the beating it would otherwise get, there's a valid argument for asserting that in mixed terrain, a good full-suspension bike can be as fast as any other mountain bike.

Just keep in mind that the full-suspension bike does require more meticulous maintenance and cleaning in order to keep the system functioning properly. The bushings of the rear pivot points should be overhauled

one to three times annually, depending on the amount of hard riding you do. Either take the bike to the bike shop or learn to do that work yourself, following the instructions in Chapter 9,

Four-bar linkage bikes tend to be heavier due to the large number of links and pivots. On the other hand, they are more responsive, providing you keep them properly adjusted and maintained.

THE GT I-DRIVE SYSTEM

Essentially, this GT proprietary suspension design is similar to a single-pivot system. However, it differs from the basic single-pivot design in that the rear wheel's path of travel follows an arc going up almost vertically (see Fig. a). This difference is due to the use of an eccentric device with the little "dog bone" attached to it.

The dog bone is the connection between the main frame and the eccentric piece. When the rear triangle suspension is activated (see figure B.), the dog bone pulls the bottom brackets forward and down. This is the clever trick which GT uses to eliminate the major drawbacks of the unified rear triangle design (i.e. its lack of responsiveness when the rider is standing on the pedals). In addition, the distance between the seat and the bottom bracket remains constant, even when the suspension is activated Finally, the suspension is separated from the drive train—consequently it eliminates the irritating pedal kickback or the power-consuming effects of the suspension when accelerating uphill (called the "anti-squat" effect).

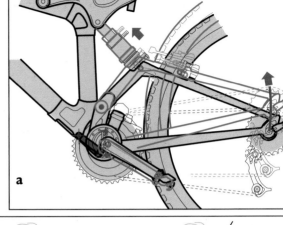

a

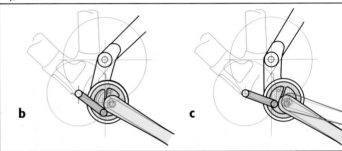

b   c

With a relatively complicated design, GT managed to develop its proprietary suspension system, the I drive. Its major advantage is that the pivot point for the rear triangle is exactly in the center of the bottom bracket. Its disadvantages lie in the fact that additional elements are required, such as the dog bone and the proprietary bottom bracket housing. Consequently, this design is relatively maintenance-intensive—and rather expensive.

The I-Drive, which is a GT proprietary rear suspension arrangement, is an attempt to combine the advantages of the single-pivot swingarm with those of the four-bar linkage suspension: low weight and sensitive response.

keeping in mind that this is a job for which you should allow yourself about five hours time—and a well equipped workshop with the requisite tools, for which you are referred to Chapter 5.

There are a number of different methods to achieve the rear suspension of the full-suspension bike. The main distinction is between single-pivot and four-pivot systems. It is not always easy to decide which is best, not only because different manufacturers have their own variations on these two general themes, but also because there is great variation in quality and attention to detail.

When trying to decide for yourself, first define the kind of riding you will do with your full-suspension bike: Do you want the fastest bike possible for downhill, freeride, or double slalom competition? Or do you need it for cross-country competition? Or do you want more comfort and reliability for non-competitive long-distance cross-country touring, or perhaps just for short trips on trails close to home? The table on page 13 provides specific advice on this subject.

One important criterion has remained valid for full-suspension bikes as it has been for all mountain

On the basis of many years of testing and riding, the author and his fellow-editors have defined the different categories of mountain bike use and matched them up with the characteristics of the different types of suspension. You can use these guidelines to select the type that best matches your riding style.

CROSS-COUNTRY AND MARATHON

Select this category for ambitious fast riding styles, including actual competition. For this use, speed and responsiveness of the bike are more important than the rider's physical comfort—efficiency is

HARDCORE FREERIDE BIKE

Not so long ago, the bikes in this category would have been considered all-out downhill bikes. They have lots of suspension travel—optimized geometry for downhill riding and for the roughest terrain: all that calls for a rugged construction of frame and components.

DIRT RIDING SUSPENSION BIKES

Dual Slalom, Bike Cross, Trials, those are the categories of use for this type of bike. Give it a trashing on a BMX course or around the neighborhood. These bikes have a very short and upright frame geometry, with wide and high handlebars that are mounted close to the rider on a stubby stem.

DOWNHILL BIKE

Real championship bikes that will allow you to throw yourself downhill like there's no tomorrow—but they aren't much fun to pedal uphill. Typically, they have only a single (large) chain-ring and a weight of around 18 kg (40 lbs). They all have a very short and upright geometry that puts the rider far back. Their suspension travel can be as much as 8 inches for the ultimate in downhill speed and comfort.

There are significant differences between full-suspension bikes with respect to their rate of suspension travel, which makes them suitable for different purposes. Additionally, enduro and downhill bikes tend to be heavier.

what counts. Low weight, a low and stretched-out rider position, and high-quality components are what you should be looking for.

ENDURO

For this kind of use, you need a bike that will perform under the widest range of conditions. You want a bike that goes downhill like a hardcore freerider, uphill like a mountain goat. Enduros call for full-suspension bikes with the optimal all-round qualities. The lightest possible frame construction, a balanced riding posture, and lightweight wheels ensure an enjoyable ride in every type of terrain. The most recent trend amongst high-end bikes in this category is the use of a level-equalizing system, which allows you to tune the bike's suspension to the specific terrain for the ride.

A typical enduro full-suspension bike is built for comfort. Strong and with lots of travel, but not too heavy, which would spoil the fun going uphill.

bikes since the beginning of the sport: Within a given type, the lighter the bike, the more expensive it will be, and the nicer it will be to ride, providing it does not go at the expense of quality.

Especially in the realm of full-suspension bikes, it is important that the critical moving parts of the suspension system, though light, must be of substantial quality, and that can only be achieved with the use of strong lightweight materials, which in turn are much more expensive than similar-looking versions made of more mundane materials.

The choice of suspension method largely affects the frame weight: the more pivot points, the heavier the frame will be, especially if high-quality machine bearings are used at the pivot points. Consequently, it should be obvious that if you want to minimize the bike's weight above all other things, you should look for a single-pivot system. If, on the other hand, comfort or downhill characteristics are more important for you, a four-pivot system will more likely be what you should be looking for.

The type of rear suspension that works with three pivots in the rear triangle has lost ground against the one-and four-pivot systems, because in the former, the shock absorber is a load-bearing component of the rear frame, carrying transverse forces, while most shock absorbers are not really designed for this kind of use and start to leak under these circumstances. Similarly, the once popular unified rear triangle design is no longer in production with most of

Modern shock units are sophisticated products that contribute significantly to a bike's riding characteristics.

Choose your mountain bike for the kind of use you have in mind. Select a freeride bike if you enjoy doing trials and singletrack riding.

the major full-suspension bike manufacturers. Just the same, the advantage of this design is its simplicity, which makes this type quite suitable for moderate riders who tend to stay in the saddle most of the time. The table on page 13 summarizes the various characteristics, advantages, and disadvantages of the different suspension systems in use today.

The correct choice and adjustment of the rear spring element is particularly important for the full suspension bike, especially in the case of four-pivot systems, where otherwise a see-saw effect could result when applying force to the pedals. Important factors in this regard are the rider's weight, his or her riding style (i.e., smooth,

gradual application of power versus short burst of power), the frame geometry, and the dimensional constraints of the frame at the location where the shock unit is mounted.

These shock units may either be based on a compressed air cartridge or a steel coil spring, and you will find more information on both systems in Chapters 9 and 10. Before buying a new bike (or, when upgrading an existing bike by replacing the shock unit), by all means ask for advice at the bike shop to further help you decide which type will best meet your needs. Some dealers even have a number of trial units (complete bikes and/or shock units) available to test before you buy.

QUICK SUSPENSION TEST

Here are three tips to help you test the rear suspension before leaving the showroom. But beware: Even if you like what you establish in this test, you'll still want
to do a real test ride before you buy the bike.

I. BRAKE BACKLASH TEST

This test is useful to establish whether there will
be brake backlash—which can stiffen the suspension while braking, resulting in reduced traction and comfort going downhill. To test, block
the rear wheel by pulling the brake lever for the
rear brake (usually the one on the right). Now
push firmly down on the seat while keeping the
brake lever pulled and check how the rear suspension reacts. For downhill comfort, you want
a system that does not "stiffen up" when the
brake lever is pulled as compared to the same
test without brake engagement.

2. PEDAL BACKLASH TEST

Systems with too much pedal backlash become really hard to
pedal and control in rough terrain. To check for pedal backlash,
first engage the smallest chainring and then push down hard on
the seat. If the cranks
jump backward as you do
so, you have a bike with
pedal backlash—not good
if you want to pedal the
bike through rough terrain.

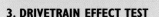

3. DRIVETRAIN EFFECT TEST

If your pedaling motion influences the suspension too much, you'll find it hard to accelerate
the bike. To test for this, place the bike with
the front wheel against a wall and place the
pedals in the horizontal ("quarter-to-nine")
position. Now place one foot on the forward

pedal and one hand on the seat, then step up and let your entire body weight rest on that forward pedal and the
saddle. If the suspension "stiffens up" markedly, you've got a bike with too much pedaling effect, and you'll find
the suspension significantly reduced when accelerating or forcefully pedaling uphill.

3 ALL ABOUT FRAMES AND COMPONENTS

Selecting a new mountain bike, or upgrading your existing machine, may seem to be a daunting task. There are so many different makes and models available, so many different materials, and so many different components to choose from. And then the prices—you can get what looks like a fully equipped mountain bike at a "big box" store for around $100, and the bike trade offers models all the way up to $5,000. So what's the difference? It helps if you understand the terminology—and the bike trade has developed its own "insider" lingo, a peculiar variant of the English language as spoken in California, enriched by the home-brewed terms created by the Japanese and Taiwanese component manufacturers. As we describe the parts of the bike, try to make yourself familiar with the names of those parts.

THE FRAME

Think of the frame as the equivalent of the chassis of an old-fashioned car—the backbone of the vehicle, to which all the other components are attached. Taken together, frame and components determine the bike's characteristics, and its quality and durability. By now, the majority of mountain bikes are based on an aluminum frame, although steel is still used (and by no means inferior—see the "Frame Materials" box on page 24).

When replacing a bike, whether in its entirety or just the frame, you'll first have to decide on the frame material to select. It gets more complicated when it comes down to selecting the various component groups, or "gruppos," as they are called these days. Components are all the parts other than the frame itself—wheels, crankset, seat, gears, brakes, etc. (and most of these components themselves are actually made up of several smaller components).

The frame is the backbone of your mountain bike, while the components define the way it's equipped. Which frame material and components you select depends on the kind of use you'll give your bike—and on how much money you have available.

Usually, gears and drivetrain components come from the same manufacturer (usually Shimano, although there still are a few other manufacturers of such items) and from the same gruppo—think of a gruppo as a "component package" of items matched to each other. Shimano has a whole range of gruppos, ranging from the quite functional but somewhat crudely finished Alivio, Acera, and Altus found on cheap bikes to the beautifully finished and lightweight XTR found on the most expensive bikes. Other manufacturers include SR SunTour and SRAM, both of which at present seem to make mainly components for lower-end bikes. Consult the table marked "Component Gruppo Overview" on page 23 to find which gruppo you should expect to find on bikes in a certain price category.

Now back to the frame. What material you choose depends on your personal preference and the kind of use you have in mind. Here are a few suggestions to help you determine the quality of the frame. The most important criteria are the tube material and the quality of assembly, which can be judged by the appearance of the welds that hold the tubes together (or in the case of a lugged steel frame, the appearance of the lug-to-tube connection). In the case of a steel frames, the names of high-quality tubing manufacturers include True Temper, Columbus, Reynolds, Tange, and Ritchey. Their decals attached to the frame assures you of the quality these manufacturers offer. Read the label carefully so you know just which particular type of tubing is used, because each of these manufacturers makes tubing sets at different prices and quality levels.

One of the buzz-words you'll find on those labels is "butted," which refers to an increased wall thickness near the ends, where needed, as opposed to the middle section. References to triple- and quadruple-butted tubing, though linguistically curious (how many butts, or ends, can a tube have if not two?), refer to the number of different wall thicknesses used through the length of the tube. More seems to be better, because it means the manufacturer has done everything possible to save weight where the extra thickness is not needed, while reinforcing the tubes at points where the higher forces are applied or where the welding process requires it.

Whereas aluminum frames are invariably welded, steel frames are either made with lugs or fillet brazed. The latter process looks a bit like welding, but here the tubes are connected with a different, lower-melting-point material that fills in the tiny gaps between the tubes and forms a perfect bond—look for perfectly smooth transitions without gaps for a high-quality frame made this way. Lugs, hardly used any more these days, are exterior connection pieces, but these too can reveal the quality—again the smoothness of the transition is a telltale feature.

Aluminum tubing is also distinguished by a decal disclosing the manufacturer and the type of tubing used, Easton being one of the major high-quality players in the field. Again the number of butts quoted suggests how much effort has gone into keeping the frame as light as possible without sacrificing strength where needed.

The parts of a component gruppo include crankset, wheel hubs, rear cog cassette, derailleurs, and brakes, the latter two with their operating levers.

There are a number of different aluminum alloys in use (an alloy is a mixture of a metal with some other material, and in fact they're all alloys—even the cheapest aluminum and steel frames are made of some kind of alloy). Refer to the box marked "Frame Materials" on page 24 for detailed information regarding the respective merits of the various aluminum alloys currently in use for bicycle frames. Perhaps you should shy away from frames without any decals identifying their manufacturer because they are likely to be of inferior quality. On a high-quality, high-price bike, the bike shop should be able to identify the characteristics of the materials used, which can't be done if they're not even disclosed by the bike's manufacturer.

Let's take a look at the weld seams on those aluminum frames. They should be consistent and regular in appearance, without interruptions, or gaps, or globs. Because the main rear suspension pivots are often welded on to the frame close to the bottom bracket, this is a good place to examine their weld quality. Sometimes the "natural" appearance of the weld seams are obscured by cosmetic tricks such as grinding or filling them in—if they look too smooth to identify their characteristics, it's impossible to judge their quality. Many experts claim that grinding down a weld seam to make it look smoother is detrimental to the integrity of the welds because it often also cuts into the tubes. On the other hand, since this method has been successfully used by very reputable manufacturers, such as Gary Klein, it may be perfectly safe if done well.

On the subject of finish, although some aluminium frames are either left bare or polished to a nice shine and then treated with transparent lacquer, most frames are painted. A more durable finish is powder coating, which generally leaves a slightly less smooth, shiny finish but is very hard and wear resistant, and actually adds a little weight. Before you buy a bike or a component, you can of course only judge the quality of the finish visually, whereas hard use is going to tell for sure how resistant it is: A high-quality paint finish will still look good even after a couple of years' hard riding.

If you buy a frame, rather than a complete bike, and equip it with components of your own choice, you should make sure that the screw threads for the bottom bracket and the derailleur hanger are not painted inside. If they are, you should get the shop to "clean up" those screw threads with a thread cutter before you try to install your components. Also the bearing cups for the steering—the headset bearings—are also best installed by the shop where you buy the frame, because these operations require special tools that are too expensive for the amount of use you'd get out of them.

You should also consider warranties. Although many manufacturers give a general "lifetime" warranty on the frame, it's often a matter of "what the large print giveth, the small print taketh:" You may find that that cherished warranty may be encumbered by so many limitations that it doesn't cover the kind of uses you have in mind—like racing or jumping. Whatever you do get by way of warranty, make sure the dealer stamps the card and fills out the date of purchase, and that you fill out the rest and mail it in. Keep your copy in a safe place together with the store receipt.

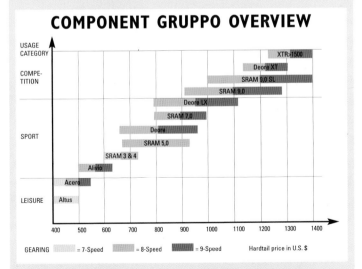

A line-up of full-suspension bike frames. Although aluminum alloy is the material of choice for most mountain bikes these days, other materials, such as carbon fiber and titanium are also used. Oversized frame tubes and hefty weld seams provide the required strength and stiffness.

Overview of the hierarchy of Shimano and SRAM component gruppos ranked by price of the bicycle on which they're used. Some gruppos are available with 8- or 9-speed rear cassettes, while these days 7-speed versions are only used on low-end bikes

COMPONENTS

Once you have selected a frame or a particular bike, you'll have to make some decisions about the componentry. Even if you buy a

ALUMINUM

This is the first choice for mountain bike frames these days, especially amongst full-suspension bikes. It will actually not be pure aluminum but some aluminum alloy that is stronger than the pure metal. Amongst the high-quality alloys commonly used are the 6061 and 7020 alloys. If there's a T behind the number, it will have been heat treated to compensate for the weakening effect of the welds. After the frame is welded, it is subjected to a sequence of predetermined temperatures over specific times. The major aluminum frame tubing manufacturers are the American companies Easton and Alcoa. Meanwhile also manufacturers who have traditionally made high-quality steel alloy frame tubing—includings Tange, Reynolds, Oria, and Columbus—now make aluminum frame tubing. Experienced manufacturers like Cannondale, Klein, Trek, etc. pretty much give you the assurance that these frames have been well made, and for now, the best assurance for quality still is probably that it's actually made by the manufacturer himself (in the USA) rather than somewhere in mainland China.

STEEL

The heyday of steel seems to have past with the waning years of the 20th century. In the U.S., Trek (the company who owns several brands, including Fisher, Klein, and LeMond) also had an all-steel line called Bontrager, started by mountain bike pioneer and prolific inventor/designer Keith Bontrager, but in recent years, that name only appears on some of Trek's in-house components. Just the same, Chrome-Molybdenum steel (often referred to as "Cro-Mo") is a superbly suitable material, especially with the wide range of wall-thickness variations that has been offered until recently. Frames made with steel tubing invariably have (and need) tubes with smaller diameters than those used on aluminum frames. The tubes are either butt-welded together, fillet-brazed together with smooth "lug-less" transitions, or connected by means of lugs into which the ends of the tubes fit and are brazed. Within any one price cagetory, steel frames—if you can find them—are a really good choice, especially if you're not turned on too much by the oversized optics of current aluminum frames.

CARBON FIBER

Formerly only used for exotic prototypes and super-fancy machines built in small numbers, carbon fiber has recently become a more common frame material for mountain bikes, especially for full-suspension machines. The carbon fiber material is woven together in the shape of mats that are placed over a form and then embedded in a thermo-setting resin compound. The difference between carbon fiber and so-called thermoplastic materials lies merely in the type of binder material used: Thermoplastics soften when heated, whereas thermosetting materials remain hard even if heated subsequently. Major manufacturers, such as Giant, GT, and Trek, have started to use this material extensively enough to have gained a lot of experience. Both the exact materials used and the production process are often proprietary to the individual manufacturer. In addition to its lower weight, carbon fiber can be made to offer more damping and elasticity than other frame materials (or, depending on just how they are dimensioned, they can be made stiffer). A disadvantage is that certain parts, such as the bottom bracket shell and the headset, have to be embedded, and these locations are so highly stressed that the material may get deformed or even crack.

TITANIUM

This exotic metal is the classical choice for really high-end hardtail bikes. The material is lighter than steel (though heavier than aluminum), and its mechanical properties are better than those of aluminum. Titanium doesn't rust either, so it does not need to be painted, giving it a look all its own. It's possible to make a very resilient and lightweight bike frame, and yes, it will be expensive, although titanium frame prices are coming down with Chinese imports reaching the U.S. market. The material is hard to work with, and in some cases the flexibility that seems so nice at first backfires by resulting in a frame that's laterally not as rigid as it should be. Some manufacturers, like Scott Nicol, use the material's flexibility in the rear triangle to produce a "soft-tail." Even considering the reduced prices in recent years, titanium will probably remain out of reach for the average cyclist who's looking for the most bike for his buck.

complete bike, you may well want to replace certain parts by other makes or models, and you may want some additional items that don't come standard on the bike of your choice. What quality of componentry you choose should depend primarily on the way you plan to use the bike, rather than the amount of money you want to spend: There's no point in "saving" money on components that are not up to the task, which you will later have to replace by more suitable items.

If you plan to use the bike only for easy tours and in fair weather, you'll find that the cheaper Shimano gruppos Alivio, Acera, and Altus (or equivalents made by other manufacturers), are quite adequate. If you're more ambitious, you will be well served by components from the Deore and Deore LX lines, while for competitive use, you should not shy away from the relatively high price of the XT and XTR gruppos.

tected against the penetration of water and dirt, and consequently last much longer under adverse conditions. You will also find that the more expensive gear and brake components fit more accurately and are easier to adjust.

might be led to assume the bike is equipped entirely with that level of components. However, when examining the other components, which are all less obvious, you may establish that they are all from lower grade gruppos. And

Aluminum frames are welded using TIG welding equipment in countries like the U.S., Taiwan, and Germany, that's still done by hand to assure a high-quality weld, which you can recognize by the regularity of the resulting weld seam.

actually, it's less obvious parts like hubs, crankset, headset, and pedals where quality matters most. Make sure you know what you're getting by checking out each of the components. To give an example, if your hubs give up the ghost in heavy use, you'll have to replace or rebuild the entire wheels, which is either very expensive or very time consuming (and consequently just as expensive if you have to pay someone at the bike shop to do that work for you.

The bottom bracket and the headset are equally important. If either of them gives out, you'd be faced with a job that requires special tools or you'll have to

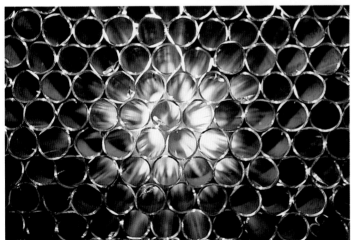

Aluminum, steel, or titanium tubes are used to build up the bicycle's frame. Tubes are available in different alloys, diameters, and wall thicknesses.

Although initially the operation of brakes and gears of the cheaper gruppos will be practically as good as it is for the more expensive equivalents, you'll find that the expensive gruppos are not only lighter, but also much better pro-

One problem you may encounter is that the bike manufacturers mix components from different gruppos. They may install a relatively high-end rear derailleur (which is the first thing most people notice), and you take the entire bike to the workshop to have it replaced for you. Make sure you get one that is up to heavy-duty offroad use, if that's what you plan to do with your bike.

Considering that there are well over 1,000 different models of mountain bikes on the market in the U.S. alone, not to mention the many options of combining one of many available frames with your own choice of componentry, there is more than enough to choose from—too much perhaps. But you can relax, because it's not as though there's only one right bike for your use: You'll find that there are quite a number of bikes made by different manufacturers that will satisfy your needs.

The quality of the paint finish can only be judged visually. Powder coating is slightly heavier and usually less shiny, but it's more durable than conventional paint finishes. Powder coating is also said to be less harmful to the environment.

use—it's what you'll need to keep up with experienced riders and it will allow you to keep control over the bike even when it gets quite rough.

If you plan to ride more than once a week and in any kind of

As a matter of fact, although you can still spend up to $5,000 for an out-and-out full-suspension downhill bike, the price of very satisfactory machines suitable for most competitive uses keeps coming down from year to year.

A technical delicacy: carbon fiber frame bonded to aluminum lugs.

PRICE CATEGORIES

The lowest price that will get you an acceptable mountain bike is around $400 (that's in the U.S.— figure the equivalent plus about 20% VAT in other countries, but don't envy us who do live in the U.S., because here the sales tax gets added to the list price). Anything cheaper—and cash-and-carry stores are full of cheaper bikes—is worthless for serious off-road use.

You should expect to pay at least $500 for a bike that satisfies slightly more ambitious

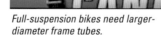

Full-suspension bikes need larger-diameter frame tubes.

weather, plan to spend about $700 for a bike with a well-built frame, Shimano DeOre LX components, and a oil-damped suspension fork.

If you're prepared to go all the way to $1,000, you should be able to get a high-quality hardtail or an adequate full-suspension bike suitable for anything short of competitive riding.

HARDTAIL SAVINGS

If you're spending $1,000, you may think you'd be crazy to get a hardtail as long as you can get a pretty nice full-suspension bike for the same money. Yet there are reasons to choose the hardtail. First off, it will be noticeably lighter than a full-suspension bike in the same price category. But you can also expect to get a higher quality level of components. What you can expect in a hardtail for this kind of money is a high-quality lightweight aluminum frame with a really nice suspension fork and a Shimano DeOre LX or even XT gruppo with very nice V-brakes, be they from Shimano or their equivalents made by Tektro, Avid, or DiaCompe. In fact, some bikes in this category come with hydraulic brakes or disk brakes. Perhaps you want to forego the latter, once you realize that the money spent on "flashy" disk brakes is saved somewhere else, and after all, V-brakes are quite adequate for most uses, (it's only in rain and snow where disk brakes perform better).

Once you get up to $1,200, you're talking high-end, at least as long as you stick with a hard-tail. You'll get a super frame with "aggressive" geometry, suitable for competitive use. Your components should be Shimano's XT, and your fork should be top-notch, at least a Rock Shox Judy or equivalent from another top brand like Manitou or Marzocchi, with smooth hydraulic damping.

In this same price category, you will also find nice full-suspension bikes, on which the quality of the frame and of the rear suspension are the most critical items. As long as that's taken care of, you may be satisfied with a little less fancy components (e.g. Shimano Deore), because you'll be able to upgrade some of the components later, while retaining the nice frame with the rear suspension. One thing to make up your mind about right away is disk brakes: it's a real hassle to install disk brakes on a bike initially equipped with conventional rim brakes, whereas they're almost guaranteed to be trouble-free if they've been installed on the bike by the manufacturer.

It's only once you pass the $1,500 point that you can expect top-quality full-suspension technology on a bike that's equipped with very functional and durable Deore LX or XT components. The sky is the limit at the top end of full-suspension mountain bikes, but once you get beyond $2,500, you're not so much paying for function as for "wow." You'll see some almost irrelevant weight savings due to the use of exotic materials like titanium or carbon fiber. Of course, any elaborate hand-made modifications also tend to push the price up into the stratosphere pretty quickly.

- **BONDED:** Essentially glued, as used on some frame joints on aluminum and carbon fiber frames.
- **BOTTOM BRACKET:** The short and stubby tube at the lowest point of a frame that holds the crankset.
- **BUTTED:** Variable wall thickness of a frame tube. The frame tube walls can be thinner in the middle section to save weight, but thicker at the ends to provide the strength and weldability where needed.
- **CARTRIDGE BEARING, OR SEALED BEARING:** Machine-type self-contained bearing running either on balls, pins ("needles"), or rollers.
- **CHAIN STAYS:** The set of horizontal tubes between the bottom bracket and the dropouts for the rear wheel axle.
- **CHAIN SUCK DEVICE:** An additional plate connected to the frame near the bottom bracket that serves to prevent the chain from getting stuck between the small chainring and the frame.
- **CNC:** Computer Numerically Controlled, which is a modern manufacturing technique for machined parts.
- **CRO-MO OR CHROME-MOLY:** Chrome-molybdenum steel, i.e. a high-strength steel alloy containing small percentages of chromium and molybenum.
- **DOWN TUBE:** The diagonal tube that connects the bottom of the steering tube with the bottom bracket.
- **DROPOUT:** U-shaped ends of the frame's rear triangle (rear) and fork (front) to which the wheels are installed.
- **FILLET BRAZING:** Technique for joining (steel or titanium) frame tubes directly.
- **FULL-SUSPENSION:** Bicycle with front and rear suspension; frame with rear suspension and designed to be used with a front suspension fork.
- **JOURNAL BEARING:** Method of making parts that can rotate, or pivot, relative to each other around a pin and a bushing rather than a ball bearing.
- **GUSSET:** Reinforcing piece that is installed on points of the frame that are highly stressed.
- **HARDTAIL:** Mountain bike frame without rear suspension.
- **HORST LINK:** A pivoting link plate on the chain stays just before the dropout to which the seat stays are connected by means of a pivot, as used on some high-end full-suspension models. Allows the rear triangle to pivot in the way of a parallelogram.
- **MAIN FRAME:** Forward portion of the frame, usually consisting of head tube, top tube, seat tube, down tube, and bottom bracket. On full-suspension bikes, it's the part of the frame that does not move up and down with the rear wheel.
- **MONOCOQUE:** One-piece frame, usually consisting either of one very large-diameter tube or a welded or bonded structure that integrates head tube, seat tube, and bottom bracket.
- **OVERSIZED:** Tubes with a diameter that's bigger than normal for increased rigidity. These days, practically all (aluminum) frames use what was still considered oversized around 1985.
- **REAR TRIANGLE:** Rearward part of the frame, usually consisting of chain stays, seat stays, and rear dropouts. On full-suspension bikes, this is the part of the frame that moves.
- **SEAT STAYS:** The almost diagonal tubes that connect the top of the seat tube with the rear dropouts.
- **SEAT TUBE:** The vertical tube between the bottom bracket and the point where the seat post is installed.
- **SINGLE-PIVOT SWINGARM:** Type of full-suspension frame with a single pivot point for the rear triangle.
- **SOFTTAIL:** Mountain bike frame with a flexible bumper between the top of the chainstays and the seat post, using the flexibility of the chain stays to soften the ride. Mainly used on (some) titanium frames.
- **STEERING TUBE:** The short and stubby vertical tube at the front of the bike, which holds the front forks and handlebars.
- **STW RATIO:** Stiffness-to-weight ratio. The higher this figure the better.
- **SWEET SPOT:** A relatively high pivot point for single-pivot rear suspension systems that serves to prevent the kickback effect when pedaling uphill from a standing position.
- **TIG WELDING:** Tungsten Inert Gas welding, meaning that the weld point is protected against the corrosive effect of the air during welding.
- **TOP TUBE:** The horizontal tube between the top of the steering tube and the seat tube
- **VPP:** Virtual Pivot Point, i.e. the effective point that can be considered the point around which the rear wheel pivots. It can be placed far forward by means of a clever configuration of the pivots and links that make up the rear triangle to achieve the desired effect of the wheel going up and down vertically as much as possible.

4 UNDERSTANDING FRAME GEOMETRY

You've made your decision: you know which bike you want. Now you're at the bike shop and it's a matter of making sure that bike actually fits you properly. Think of it as buying shoes—if they don't fit properly, you'll be miserable walking in them forever after. To make sure you'll be comfortable on the bike, this chapter will help you select a bike with a frame with the right size and geometry.

Even though there has been a trend, especially in low-end mountain bikes, toward a more upright and presumably more comfortable seating position, a beginner rarely feels really comfortable on—and especially after—the first really demanding ride. Try to prevent that effect by setting up the bike precisely to match your needs beforehand.

After many years in which most mountain bikes were sold for a stretched-out seating position, the manufacturers have finally decided to abandon this trend, which is really only good for riding downhill and for racing, and offer bikes with a shorter reach. On new bikes, that's achieved in part by making the top tube shorter than had been the trend. Otherwise, and if the bike's still one of those long ones, it can be achieved by providing a shorter handlebar stem, and if you can't find such a bike on the sales floor, ask to have the overly long stem replaced by a shorter, higher one to match your needs. The advantages are manifold: In the first place, your lower back won't hurt; secondly, visibility is increased because it will be easier to look straight ahead rather than at your front wheel. That's good for your comfort and safety, even on downhill sections. The only drawback of this position is that the bike may be harder to ride up steep climbs, because the front end of the bike tends to lift off the ground. But, since you'll only

Everybody is an individual, with physical proportions that differ from those of most other people, even if they are of the same size. Consequently everyone needs a bike that's either built or set up individually to match the rider's needs.

be riding such sections for minor distances, even in the mountains, it should not deter you from this position.

FRAME SIZE AND SEAT HEIGHT

The most important criterion when choosing a bike that fits is the frame size. This size is usually measured as the distance between the center of the bottom bracket and the top of the seat tube. This dimension should be such that it relates correctly to your leg length. To measure your leg length, establish the "inseam length," which is the distance between the ground and the highest point between your legs. Stand against the wall in bare feet with legs straight and the feet about 2 inches apart, then place e.g. a flat, rectangular piece of wood or plastic the size of a clipboard between you legs until just before it hurts, and pushed flush against the wall. Keep it in place and draw a line where the top reaches the wall, and measure the distance between the floor and this point. Measure in cm or inches: that's your inseam size.

A commonly used formula to establish the optimum frame size is 0.57 times inseam length, which gives you a frame size in cm if you measured in cm, and one in inches if you measured in inches. To convert your cm-measure to inches, multiply by 0.4; to convert an inch dimension to cm, multiply by 2.5.

So, if you measured a leg length of 85 cm (34 in.), you'll probably be comfortable on a bike with a frame that's 85 x 0.57 = 48 cm, or in inches 34 x 0.57 = 19 in. That's just a starting point, which should be seen as the midpoint of a range that extends about 1½ in. both ways. You may well have reasons to get a bike that's a bit smaller or bigger. If you ride a lot on technical trails,

you'll probably be better off with a slightly smaller bike, whereas someone who goes on long tours may want one that's a bit bigger.

Now the seat has to be placed in the right position. When riding, you should be able to almost stretch the legs fully when the pedal is in the lowest position. The best way to establish this

A longer stem, i.e. one with more reach, and a longer top tube result in a forward-leaning, stretched out position, which is comfortable only for riders with years of experience.

seat height is by sitting on the bike while holding onto a vertical surface (either a post or a door opening), and pedaling backward with your heels (wearing flat-soled shoes) on the pedals. If you can stretch your leg all the way this way without having to rock from side to side, you've found the right seat height.

TOP TUBE LENGTH

The second most important dimension is the distance between the seat and the handlebars, and in terms of frame size, that will be largely a matter of top tube length, i.e. the distance between the center of the seat and the head tube. Although that top tube isn't physically present on many modern full-suspension bikes, the horizontally measured distance between the center of the seat post and the center of the head tube is still referred to as such. There's no convenient

A short top tube and a stem with less reach result in a more upright rider position, which is more comfortable for all but the most aggressive riding styles (Especially suitable if you carry a backpack).

formula to relate this dimension to your physical dimensions. However, the test editors for mountain bike magazines have come up with a reliable method based on their experience with literally hundreds of bikes and dozens of test riders. Their findings are summarized in the table on page 33. As you can see there, the optimum top tube length depends not only on your physique, but also on the kind of riding you plan to do: longer top tubes for more aggressive riding, shorter for more comfortable touring. Again, as in the case of the seat tube length, or nominal frame size, think of it as a range rather than as a single exact dimension.

Even when you have established the correct top tube length, because your torso, your arms, or both may be of such a length that a longer or shorter top tube is more comfortable. Sit on the bike with the seat adjusted to the correct height and reach for the handlebars. It should be possible to have a slight angle at the elbows. If you find yourself stretching too much for comfort, select either a bike with a shorter top tube or the same frame with a shorter handlebar stem. If you feel you're sitting too close in, select either a longer frame or the same frame with a longer handlebar stem (that's called a stem

with more "reach"). Usually, you can adapt almost any frame by selecting a different stem and/or a different seat post (one that places the seat further forward or back, depending on your needs).

There are handlebar stems in many different sizes, defined by their reach and a second dimension, referred to as "rise," i.e. the vertical distance (sometimes defined by the angle of the top relative to the horizontal plane). However, don't go to extremes. A stem that's shorter than about 60 mm (2¼

want it to go. A stem that's more than 120 mm (4¾ in.) long will tend to result in very sluggish steering characteristics, whereby the bike just wants to go straight and it takes considerable effort to make it turn. It's recommended to stay within the range of 70 mm (2¾ in.) to 115 mm (4¼ in.).

The seating position can also be varied by exchanging the seat post. Currently, there are two alternative systems available: Ritchey and Syncros. In the case of the Ritchey system, the top of the seat post is placed about half an inch back, which places the rider back by the same amount, giving you a greater distance between the seat and the handlebars. The Syncros system does the opposite, with the top of the seatpost placed forward by about half an inch, bringing the saddle further forward by that much and decreasing the

in.) results in very direct steering characteristics, whereby the slightest movement can make your bike go where you didn't

FRAME GEOMETRY: WHAT THO

The frame geometry is signifi-cant both for the riding, balanc-ing, steering, and braking char-acteristics of the bike and for the rider's comfort. Referring to the units shown in the illustra-tion, the following explains each dimension.

STEERER TUBE ANGLE:
Should be between 71 and 74 degrees. As the angle increases (i.e. becomes steeper), the more actively the bike reacts to steering, and shallower angles give a steadier ride.

CHAIN STAY LENGTH:
Should be between 420 and 450 mm (about 16½ and 17¾ in. respectively). Shorter chain stays improve rear wheel traction.

TOP TUBE LENGTH:
A longer top tube results in a more stretched-out riding position, while a shorter top tube allows you to sit more upright (also see the table "Top Tube Length Selection" on page 33.

FRAME SIZE:
Depends on the rider's leg length (refer to the box "Tips & Tricks" on page 30).

WHEEL BASE:
A short wheel base results in a very responsive bike that's easy to steer,

Seat height

Top tube length

Frame size

Seat tube angle

Chain stay length

Wheel base

DIMENSIONS MEAN

while a longer wheel base makes the bike easier to keep on a straight course.

HEIGHT DIFFERENCE:
The bigger the height difference, i.e. the lower the handlebars are in relation to the seat, the more aggressive the bike. Good for going fast, whereas less difference means more comfort.

SEAT HEIGHT:
The distance between the seat and the pedal in its lowest position.

SEAT TUBE ANGLE:
Usually between 71 and 74 degrees. Determines the horizontal seat position relative to the bottom bracket/crankset.

STEM REACH:
the longer the stem, i.e. more reach, the further forward you have to lean to reach it. For a more comfortable, less aggressive position, select a stem with less reach.

distance between the seat and the handlebars.

Something else that could sour your first riding experience with the new bike would be an excessive difference in height between the seat and the handlebars, with the seat high up in the air and the handlebars low down, almost beyond your reach. Although that's a nice aerodynamic position for certain kinds of fast riding or riding against a strong headwind, it's not very comfortable. This too can be solved simply by replacing the stem, this time by a model with a greater rise.

Height difference

Stem reach

Steerer tube angle

TOP TUBE LENGTH SELECTION

Use this table to determine what's the best top tube length for your physique. First measure your leg length, as explained in the box "Seat Tube Length" on page 31. This figure represents the optimum frame size (i.e. seat tube length) for you. Note that the table lists two dimensions: one for a "comfortable" riding style, the other for a "competitive" style. Choose either of these values or any intermediate value between these two extremes, depending on your preference, remembering to tend toward the bigger size if your torso and arms are shorter relative to your legs, smaller if it's the other way round.

Frame size	Leg length	Top tube competition	Top tube competition
42 cm	74 cm	530 mm	555 mm
43 cm	75 cm	533 mm	558 mm
44 cm	77 cm	536 mm	561 mm
45 cm	79 cm	540 mm	565 mm
46 cm	81 cm	544 mm	569 mm
47 cm	82 cm	548 mm	573 mm
48 cm	84 cm	553 mm	578 mm
49 cm	86 cm	558 mm	583 mm
50 cm	88 cm	564 mm	589 mm
51 cm	89 cm	570 mm	595 mm
52 cm	91 cm	576 mm	601 mm
53 cm	93 cm	582 mm	607 mm
54 cm	95 cm	590 mm	615 mm

5 WORKSHOP AND TOOLS

Maintaining and repairing your mountain bike is well within the reach of most people with a modicum of basic technical skills. A well-organized workshop and an affordable set of basic tools is all you need to get started.

Working on your own bike can be an enjoyable experience—providing you have the right tools to do the jobs you want to tackle and learn how to use them correctly. That's what will be covered in this chapter.

Before you start working on the bike, get the basic collection of tools and other workshop aids described here. Nothing is more irritating than finding halfway through a maintenance job that you don't have the tools to complete it.

When buying tools, it's important that you select high-quality tools that fit accurately, because that way you make all jobs easier on yourself and avoid damaging the bike or its parts. Don't ruin your $1,000 bike by using a cheap, poorly fitting wrench, when spending a few bucks more would have assured you of a tool that does the job accurately. Buy tools either at a specialized tool shop or a bike shop (at least insofar as they are bicycle-specific tools), not at a cheap variety store. Cheap tools are often made of metal that is too soft and gets deformed easily, which often leads to damage both of the tool and of the item you're working on.

Also make sure your tools are exactly the right size to fit the components on your bike. Essentially all mountain bikes, even U.S.-made ones, use metric screw threads for bolts and nuts and most other components, so don't use a "standard" (i.e. U.S.) size tool that seems to be "about right" but the exact mm tool.

There are a few exceptions to the mm rule, namely in the realm of large screw-threaded items like the crankset and the (now rarely used) threaded headset. However, these items need very special tools, available only in bike shops, so there's no chance of confusion. Do check to make sure that the bicycle-specific tools you buy are designed for the make and model of the components on your bike, because some of them vary from one make or model to the other.

It will be a good idea not to wait for your bike to break down but to start off with simple cleaning and preventive maintenance work. This allows you to get familiar with the bike and the tools, so you'll be much better prepared when something breaks down that does require repair work. Besides, this kind of maintenance work often prevents breakdowns alltogether, so your bike will give you more enjoyment and less frustration.

The number of tools you will need to work on your mountain bike is actually quite modest. Your home tool kit may contain some of them, like a good adjustable wrench (Crescent wrench), a hammer, and a selection of screw drivers. However, when it comes to other tools, take the trouble to go out and buy designated (metric) ones, either at a good tool shop or at a bike shop, depending on the type of tool in question.

In addition to a set of Allen wrenches in the sizes from 2.5 through 7 mm, you'll need both flat-head and Phillips head screwdrivers in small and medium sizes, and if you have disk brakes also so-called Torx wrenches, which hold their matching screws better than other types of screw heads, which is important for such delicate but firmly attached items. Make sure you get them in the right sizes to match your brakes. Regular hexagonal nuts and bolts are not used much anymore on bikes, but you'll probably still need a set of open-ended metric wrenches in sizes from 7 to 17 mm.

Although it's possible to work on most mountain bikes by placing them upside-down on seat and handlebars, you'll be in a much better position to work on it if you invest in a special work stand. Not only does the work stand hold your bike firmly in place, you can also adjust it to the right height and angle depending on what part you're working on. Whenever you have to make adjustments requiring access to the shifters or levers on the handlebars while turning the cranks, you'll thank your good foresight to have bought a work stand.

When you have to disassemble components such as suspension forks or suspension swingarms, you will need to use a rubber-capped mallet, which is available at most tool shops and automotive supply stores. A normal steel hammer, or even a plastic mallet leaves ugly dents and scratches and provides too direct an impact for such delicate work.

Other frequently used bicycle-specific tools you will need, which are available at any well-equipped bike shop, are listed below:

- Cable cutter. Don't settle for a cheap one but insist on something that the mechanics in the bike shop themselves would want to use, such as the one made by Shimano, which cuts through brake and gear cables without leaving frayed ends.
- Crank puller. It must match the make and model of the crankset on your bike.
- Spoke wrench. Make sure it's of the exact size to fit the spokes on the bike you're working on.
- Tire levers. Cheap plastic ones with a hook at the end to fit around a spoke are adequate for the relatively loosely fitting mountain bike tires (though pretty useless on tightly fitting road bike tires).
- Chain rivet tool. This too has to be selected for the exact chain that's installed on your bike (depending on the number of rear cogs, because the more cogs, the narrower the chain will be. Get the model that's small enough to take along on the bike).

Above: The work stand is an essential piece of equipment for any serious bike mechanic. Resting the bike against the work bench or placing it upside down to work on it are primitive methods that don't allow you to work accurately and efficiently. Make sure the work stand, even with the bike on it, doesn't tend to tip and that it clamps the bike securely without swivelling or tipping.

Above: Tire levers should be used for fixing flats or removing tubes or tires, even on a mountain bike with its relatively loosely fitting tires.

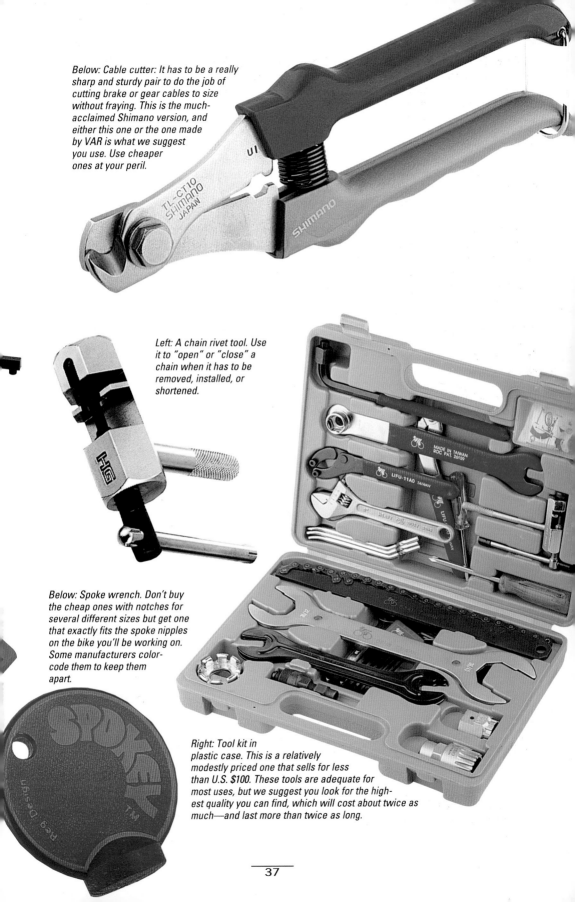

Below: Cable cutter: It has to be a really sharp and sturdy pair to do the job of cutting brake or gear cables to size without fraying. This is the much-acclaimed Shimano version, and either this one or the one made by VAR is what we suggest you use. Use cheaper ones at your peril.

Left: A chain rivet tool. Use it to "open" or "close" a chain when it has to be removed, installed, or shortened.

Below: Spoke wrench. Don't buy the cheap ones with notches for several different sizes but get one that exactly fits the spoke nipples on the bike you'll be working on. Some manufacturers color-code them to keep them apart.

Right: Tool kit in plastic case. This is a relatively modestly priced one that sells for less than U.S. $100. These tools are adequate for most uses, but we suggest you look for the highest quality you can find, which will cost about twice as much—and last more than twice as long.

Now let's look at some of the tools that you won't need quite so frequently—you'll probably go at least a 1,000 miles, or a year, under real off-road conditions before you do:

- Rear cassette tool and a "chain whip." Tools you'll need to take the cogs off the rear wheel cassette or (on an older bike with screwed-on freewheel) from the freewheel body. You'll hold one of the larger cogs steady with the chain whip, while unscrewing either the smallest cog or a special lockring that holds them together with the other tool.
- Wheel truing stand. That's what you need to hold the wheel free to rotate while you adjust the spoke tension all around with the spoke wrench to straighten a buckled wheel. Some work stands actually have an integrated truing stand.
- Bottom bracket tool. Modern mountain bikes all come with cassette bearing bottom brackets, usually by Shimano, and this tool will allow you to remove or install the complete assembly once the cranks have been removed from the bottom bracket spindle.

Finally, there are a couple of tools which you probably would only be justified buying if you work on your bike as well as on other people's. And even then, only if you have the ambition to do everything yourself, rather than (as we would generally recommend for more difficult procedures) take the bike to the bike shop when it gets tricky:

- Threadless headset tool. Use this tool to install the "star-fangled" nut that gets installed in the fork on this type of headset (and modern mountain bikes all have threadless headsets).
- Professional tubing cutter that will handle up to 1¼ in. diameter pipe. This tool, normally used by plumbers to cut water pipes, serves well to cut a fork steerer tube to size, but can also be used to reduce the size of handlebars or the length of a seatpost (pro-

viding you don't cut it so short that it can't be clamped in over at least 65 mm (2½ in).

You will find ready-made tool kits that contain all these tools, except probably the last two, by reputable manufacturers such as Park, VAR, or Trek's house brand "Wrench Force." Some of these kits are not really designed, or satisfactory, for professional use, but as long as you take the more expensive set whenever you have a chance, you're likely to get tools that stand up to the use you will be giving it. Even the expensive versions are significantly cheaper than it would be to buy each tool separately.

Below: Foot pump or, more correctly, stand pump, because you really use your hands to pump, while holding it down with your feet. Available with two different kinds of heads, one for so-called Schrader valves (like on cars and low-end bikes), the other for Presta valves (the skinny type used on road racing bikes and high-end mountain bikes)

Above: Two different sets of Allen wrenches. The compact set is handy for carrying on the bike, but the big one with the complete range from 2.5 mm through 8 mm is essential for in the workshop. The big set has a rounded Bondhus head at one end, so you can use it even when you don't have enough room to get the tool in straight.

*ove: threadless
adset tool. This is
sentially a punch with
ich you can install the curious-
shaped nut, referred to as "star-
gled nut" into the fork's steerer
e on bikes with the now almost
iversally used threadless head-
ts.*

*Above:
Combination
wrenches. Open
ended on one end, ring-shaped on the
other. Actually, you should have two complete sets in
metric sizes from 7 through 17 mm. Good ones last a lifetime and will set you back quite a bit.*

*Above: Pipe cutting tool, used to cut handlebars,
seatposts, and fork steerer tubes to size, and much
more accurately than can be done with a hacksaw.*

*Above left and right and below: Chain
whip and cassette removal tools. The
little one on the right can be used out in
the field, whereas the one below must
be clamped in by means of a vise.*

*Above:
Crank arm
puller. Unless you
have the type of cranks
that is held with a "one-key"
release, you'll need this tool to
remove the cranks off the bottom
bracket spindle. In addition, you will need a
long 8 mm Allan wrench (or for older bikes a
special skinny pipe wrench) to tighten or
loosen the bolt or the nut that holds the crank
arm on).*

6 CLEANING AND PREVENTIVE MAINTENANCE

Your bike is bound to run better and longer without trouble if you keep it in shape by regularly cleaning, lubricating, and adjusting it properly. Treat your bike to a once-a-year major overhaul, usually done in early springtime, and regular check-ups during the season to keep it tuned up at all times, minimizing the risk of trouble out on the trail.

An important step in the cleaning process during the major tune-up is to apply wax to paint and aluminum parts after they have been cleaned. That will allow water and dirt less opportunity to adhere to the bike and penetrate into sensitive areas.

If you only ride the bike occasionally and mainly in good weather, oiling the chain once a month will be all you need to do by way of regular maintenance between major overhauls. But as you ride more frequently and under harsher conditions, regular maintenance sessions become more frequent and more extensive. In that case you should at least clean and lubricate the bike after every ride in the rain (or in snow if you're in a region blessed by snowfall in winter). That only needs to take five minutes, which will pay off handsomly the next time you want to go for a ride. The dirt is still easy to remove with plain water just after the ride, whereas it's a hassle to clean a bike that's had dirt caked on for a week or so.

If you wait until the dirt has dried, you not only need much more water and other aids to get it clean, you'll also have to do more in the way of drying and lubricating the bike, because all that water and especially other cleaning aids will have penetrated into places where it does more harm then good, like inside ball bearings, brakes, and derailleurs.

When buying cleaning aids, and there are bike-specific cleaners on

Don't let dirt and corrosion get the better of your bike. You can save yourself a lot of repair work by making sure the bike is kept clean, lubricated, and well maintained. And you'll have more fun riding, because your bike won't let you down.

the market that are sold in bike shops, take the trouble to check the label to find out what's inside. Tensides, phosphates, etc. is what most manufacturers put in those bottles, and unfortunately, they're not biodegradable. One of the biggest environmental hazards is the group of detergent agents called tensides. They reduce the water's surface tension, thus enabling the water to penetrate through the dirt more readily. They break right into greasy layers, and unfortunately also into the wax you put on the bike to protect it and the lubricant in your bearings and cables. And as though tensides aren't enough, phosphates go even further in the same process of helping water penetrate and dissolve anything in its path.

Don't worry too much if you have a high-end bike, though: Most of the bearings of high-end components are reasonably well protected against the pene-

many years before they have to be replaced.

The only difference between the various cleaners on the market is the concentration of the different cleaning aids mixed in. Even minor concentrations of cleaning aids are not entirely

out resorting to those special cleaning aids.

Also be extremely careful to avoid spilling any oil when lubricating the bike. A single drop of oil can contaminate as much as 1,000 liters (260 U.S. gal.) of water. Try to catch or wipe any ex-

Chain cleaning devices with pertinent cleaning liquids make it easy to clean the chain, but they also have disadvantages: They dissolve remaining lubricant inside and make it harder for new lubricant to penetrate.

harmless to the environment, because in most cases you have little choice but let the water

Wetbrush

Handy cleaning and lubricating aid: Wash tank, wet brush, and cog cleaning brush. And to clean up your hands afterwards, there's waterless hand cleaner and hand care lotion.

tration of dirt (and to some extent of water) with rubber or butyl seals, and at least neither phosphates nor tensides destroy those materials themselves. Grease and oil don't affect those seals either, so they usually last

used to clean the bike (with every nasty product that's dissolved) run into the sewer system or straight into the ground. That's one good reason to clean your bike before it's so dirty that the job can't be done with-

cess oil, and keep separate rags for oily and greasy work. A good way to minimize the spilled oil problem is by placing a large piece of cardboard under the bike when you're working on it. After a season's worth of maintenance, you can take the cardboard and any greasy rags to a recycling center for oil products (many auto supply stores will accept those products).

A quick glance at the drivetrain reveals whether the rider treats his or her bike to such regular cleaning or not. The chain treatment described below is quite adequate to keep the chain—and the other components of the drivetrain and gearing—running smoothly. If you not only clean the chain but also protect it with wax after cleaning, your drivetrain will even keep running smoothly in the rain, without attracting more dirt.

The frame will also be grateful for a layer of protective wax, keeping its friendly new smile for many years. Oily bike care products, on the other hand, are suitable to protect screwed connections and hard-to-reach places. If you use these products over larger areas, they attract dust and quickly make things worse rather than better after a day's ride.

All this cleaning is worth every minute you spend on it. The next time you take the bike out for a ride, it will run like new. The amount spent is no greater than what you would spend on your own hygiene after a muddy ride.

CLEANING AND LUBRICATION AIDS

Conscientious care of the bike is not just a matter of keeping it looking pretty. It's also a way of keeping it working better. Here is a list of items to buy for your regular maintenance:

- Cleaning Liquid: Dissolves or softens caked-on dirt on the frame and components. After it's soaked in for some time, the mixture of dirt and cleaning liquid can easily be removed with water.

- Degreaser: Dissolves oil, grease, and greasy dirt. Especially suitable for chainrings, derailleurs, rear cogs, and for external cleaning of the chain. Can also be used to help clean other greasy components, and even for the frame in areas that tend to get greasy, such as the right-hand chainstay.

- Wax Spray: Serves to protect and seal the external surfaces of painted and bare metal parts. Suitable for the frame as well as the chain (after it has been lubricated). Its antistatic properties make it repel dust, preventing the build-up of dirt.

- Chain Cleaner: Often used in special chain cleaning gadgets, but perfectly suitable for independent use. It has a highly degreasing effect, which means it tends to remove the lubricant remnants inside the chain bushing as well if you apply it too generously (as the special gadgets invariably do) and some of the liquid stays inside, making it harder for fresh lubricant to penetrate. The best way to clean the chain is by soaking a cloth in chain cleaner; then grab around the chain with the cloth in your hand, pulling the chain through to apply it.

- Cleaning Oil: Provides corrosion protection for screw-thread connections and inaccessible parts. Just like wax, it leaves a protective film, which, however, isn't exactly antistatic: Left on too generously, it attracts dirt. Excellent for "mothballing" the bike before the onset of winter, if you live somewhere where winter riding is not an option.

- Silicon Oil: Very suitable for the upkeep of flexible parts made of rubber, butyl, or other plastics. It doesn't work as a lubricant as well as regular oils without silicon, so don't use it where lubrication is critical, like the chain. It also repels dust.

- Lubricating Oil: Works both for lubrcating and to prevent corrosion. Suitable for the chain (after cleaning) and pivot points. Oils with better penetrating properties are more effective at reaching out-of-the-way places like inside the chain links; however, that goes at the expense of their lubricating properties. Additives like Teflon improve their effectiveness.

1. CLEANING

Use a cleaner in a spray bottle, and check the directions for use. Unless, otherwise stated, first spray the entire bike with the spray bottle of cleaning liquid, applying it a bit more thoroughly in places where the dirt has caked on in a thick crust. Now just let the bike stand for 15 minutes while the cleaning liquid penetrates into the dirt.

2. RINSING

The dissolved dirt can now easily be removed with water from a hose nozzle or, to conserve water, with a sponge from a bucket. As opposed to a powerful squirt of water from the hose nozzle, the sponge method is less likely to let water penetrate into places where it shouldn't, such as the bearings.

3. AFTER-TREATMENT

Dirt remnants in hard-to-reach places are best removed by means of a long, narrow dishwashing brush or with the sponge. Use a bucket of water with a few drops of cleaning liquid. Also the wheels can be made to shine like new this way.

4. THE GEARING SYSTEM

Chainrings coated with greasy dirt, rear cog cassettes, and derailleurs can be cleaned with the help of a degreaser.

Apply it sparingly from the spray bottle, allow it to penetrate, and then clean with a narrow brush. Put some degreaser in a jar and dip the brush in from time to time—but wipe the dirty brush on a rag before you dip it.

5. THE CHAIN

If the chain is covered in dirt, first try to clean it as much as possible with a brush and a mixture of water and bike cleaning solvent. An old tooth brush is quite suitable for this. Once it looks clean, use a rag that's been soaked in a degreaser to remove caked-on greasy dirt. This is adequate for a chain that's moderately greasy. You can buy special chain cleaner tools that contain a series of brushes and a bath of solvent and/or lubricant, but even these aren't the cat's whiskers because they tend to remove the useful lubricants from inside, without removing the fine dirt particles.

6. CHAIN LUBRICATION

Proper lubrication makes the chain run smoothly. Use a special chain lubricant in a drip bottle and, holding the bottle upside down to drop lubricant on the chain, while rotating the cranks so the chain receives and distributes the lubricant. It's preferable to apply the lubricant to the inside of the chain, as shown in the illustration. It's best to try and get the oil close to the link plates on either side of the chain, so the oil can penetrate inside the bushes and rollers, which doesn't happen if you apply it to the middle of the rollers and apply a drop of lubricant to the pivot pins of the derailleurs. Then let it stand overnight and then wipe any excess off with a rag. Make sure there's something like a piece of cardboard under the bike to catch any excess lubricant or cleaner.

7. CHAIN PRESERVATION

Applying chain wax spray to the chain after this will protect the chain without attracting dirt. The wax builds a thin but tough protective layer that's actually antistatic to repel dust particles. In addition, you'll have a much easier time cleaning the chain the next time that job is necessary.

8. CARE OF THE PAINTWORK

Wax also serves to protect the frame so it stays clean longer between maintenance intervals. It reduces the build-up of dirt, which doesn't adhere as easily to the smooth antistatic layer of wax as it does to bare paint. Before applying the wax, all you usually need to do is rinse the bike with a hose or with a sponge dipped in water from a bucket. Use a cotton rag to shine the wax after you've sprayed it on.

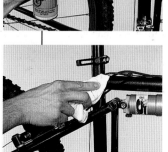

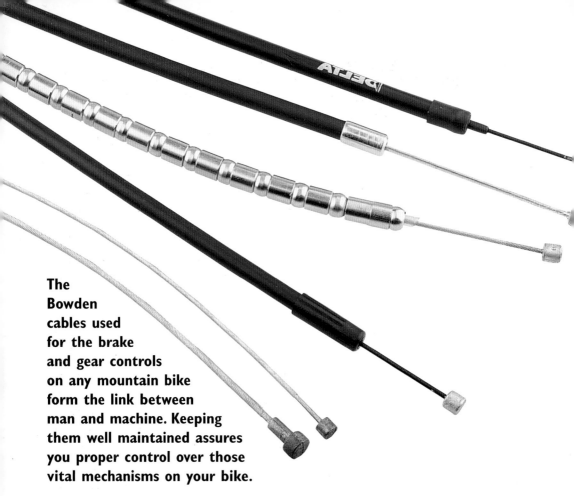

The Bowden cables used for the brake and gear controls on any mountain bike form the link between man and machine. Keeping them well maintained assures you proper control over those vital mechanisms on your bike.

1. As supplied by the manufacturer, most bikes are equipped with conventional cable systems, with the bare inner cables routed unprotected between the outer cable stops on the frame. This allows easy penetration of water and dirt inside the sections of the outer cable. Check the operation of the cables regularly as follows: First release the tension on the cable. To do that for the brake cable, disconnect the cable at the brake. For the derailleur cables, select the gears by which the chain runs over the largest chainring in front and the largest cog in the rear. This way the cable can be lifted out of the slotted cable stops at the brake levers and gear mechanisms.

Now you have access to the entire length of inner cable by sliding the sections of outer cable along to uncover different sec-

tions of inner cable. Use a rag soaked in either grease or wax to coat the unprotected inner wire. This will protect the cables against the ravages of penetrating water. No need to bother with all of this if the steel inner cable is covered by a nylon or Teflon sleeve, which serves the same purpose as lubrication does.

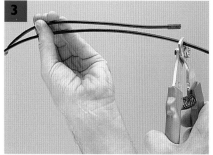

2. Treat your bike to new inner cables from time to time. That's a relatively cheap way of keeping your brakes and gears running smoothly. When you see corrosion and/or fraying of cable strands at the ends, it's time to replace them.

3. When you're having difficulty braking or shifting despite new inner cables, lubrication, and adjustment, it's time to re-place the outer cables, or cable housings. This will also be a good time to consider replacing the entire cable system by one of the closed systems that are available, which are sold as com-plete sets cut and finished to a certain length (hold it along the bike to make sure you get the right size). To replace just the outer cable, first make sure the old cables are routed optimally; if so, cut your outer cable sections to the same size; if not, make the necessary adjustments in length. Using the special cable cutters prevents frayed inner cables and hooked ends to the outer cable.

4. This is how well-routed cables look: gradual curves, not too tight, and not too generous. On suspension bikes, it's necessary to assure you cut them long enough to allow for the entire range of movement of the wheels and/or the rear triangle rela-tive to the main frame without kinking or stretching the cables.

5. Don't ask why SRAM calls this device Nightcrawler—it keeps water and dust out of the rear derailleur cable housing just as well by daylight as at night. It's a cheap but effective up-grade, because the rear derailleur, with its 9 or so different po-sitions, is very sensitive to extraneous effects, such as caused by a rough cable operation. The alternative is to replace the cables by fully closed cable systems, as described above under point 3. That's one way to make your gearing system reliable.

6. Ever jabbed yourself with one of those fraying cable strand ends? These crimp-on end caps are the way to prevent that from happening. With today's stainless steel cables, the other option of soldering the strands together is no longer easy to carry out. Place the end cap over the end of the cable and squeeze them flat in two different places along their length, using the cutting portion of pliers that are not too sharp.

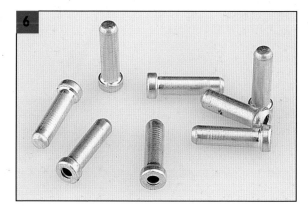

7 UNDERSTANDING SUSPENSION FORKS

Yes, suspension forks have become standard equipment on any mountain bike worthy of the name in recent years. You can take it for granted, like a saddle or handlebars. If it doesn't have a suspension fork, it isn't a mountain bike. That's because the advantages of having a front suspension far outweigh the remnants of disadvantages these devices have—like the extra weight and increased maintenance. In the first place, you get more safety because your front wheel stays in contact with the ground much better than on a bike with a rigid fork. Secondly, there's the increase in comfort due to the absorption of shocks and vibration, and increased control over the bike because your hands don't go numb.

How much suspension do you need on a mountain bike? Well, that's measured in terms of "travel," i.e. the difference in length between the compressed and relaxed positions, usually measured in mm. Whereas early suspension forks usually had 40 to 60 mm of travel, the trend has been toward more and more, and 80 mm has become the standard in recent years, while 100 mm, or 4 inches, of travel can be expected on high-end downhill and freeride bikes. For hardcore freeride and downhill use, you may even encounter forks with 110 mm of travel and more. Less travel is mainly found on models intended for cross-country racing and perhaps for people who want to save weight wherever they can.

Of the many methods introduced in the early days of mountain bike front suspension, there are three types that have survived: telescopic fork, parallelogram-linkage forks, and headtube suspension. Of these, the most common type is the telescopic suspension fork—made by companies like Rock Shox, Manitou, Marzocchi, SR SunTour, Fox, and Magura—

There's hardly a mountain bike sold without a suspension fork these days. It makes a good mountain bike even better, and a good bike ride even more enjoyable. Here's an overview of the different types to help you understand and choose the best one for your use.

and sometimes with a double or even triple-crown design for downhill bikes.

Parallelogram-linkage forks, such as those made by K2/Proflex and AMP, are much less common, but they are still around. The head tube shock, finally, has been exclusive to Cannondale for many years, and referred to as "Headshok" Unlike the other two types, the head tube suspension requires the use of a special frame with a very large-diameter headtube, which contains the suspension.

Even within each of these three general design categories, there are differences in suspension and damping technology used by different manufacturers in various models. Depending on the manufacturer's philosophy and the price category for which the fork is intended, you'll find suspension elements comprising elastomer pads, steel coil springs, or compressed air. As for damping, that can rely either on elastomer friction or oil cartridges. These days, many of the higher-end designs actually comprise a combination of different elements, such as oil-damped

compressed air in one leg and a coil spring with elastomer damping in the other—whatever the

Details like this little lubricating nipple facilitate suspension fork maintenance and increase the fork's life expectancy.

manufacturer has found to provide the optimum combination of suspension and damping characteristics for the intended use.

Much of today's bicycle suspension technology was "borrowed" from motorcycle practice. Although there are obvious similarities, there are also big differences due to the fact that on a motorcycle the machine itself is the bulk of the overall weight that has to be suspended and a few

COMPARISON OF SUSPENSION FORK SYSTEMS

TYPE	ADVANTAGES	DISADVANTAGES
Elastomer spring and damping	Light, cheap, bottom-out protection	Stiffens up in cold weather, poor damping
Steel coil spring/ elastomer damping	Responsive, bottom-out protection, adjustability	More expensive, heavier
Steel coil spring/ oil damping	Very responsive, good damping	Heavier, even more expensive
Air suspension/ oil damping	Very responsive, good damping, bottom-out protections	Expensive, hard to adjust

pounds one way or the other is no object, whereas on the bicycle, the rider's weight forms the bulk of the mass and every extra ounce of weight is watched with suspicion.

In addition to the two basic functions of "springiness" and damping, modern bicycle suspension forks are usually equipped with adjustments for the various functions to fine-tune the fork to the many variables that matter in mountain biking—rider weight, terrain roughness, riding style,

High-quality suspension forks are adjustable. This is a knob that allows adjustment of the rebound rate.

etc. In addition, lock-out or adjusting devices are now often integrated to allow the rider to make the necessary adjustments without tools, sometimes even while remaining on the bike. Lock-out levers may be mounted directly on the fork or they can be activated from the handlebars.

On many high-end forks, the range of travel can be adjusted between 60 and 110 mm by means of devices such as the U-Turn (Rock Shox) or ECC (Marzocchi). Of course, all this extra technology has its price, and a fancy suspension fork can cost a small fortune if bought individually. The answer is often to look for the ads in magazines such as *Mountain Bike Action* in the U.S., offering last year's models left over from the OEM (Original Equipment Manufacturer) market

GLOSSARY

- **AFTERMARKET KIT:** Set of parts used to modify the characteristics of a suspension fork.
- **ANTI-BOB:** Manitou's lockout system, which can be retrofitted to certain models.
- **CARTRIDGE:** enclosed, sealed cartridge usually containing hydraulic damping fluid.
- **CLIMB-IT CONTROL:** Rock-Shox's damping control knob on top of the fork crown.
- **DAMPING:** Method to reduce uncontrolled swinging motion in response to activation of the suspension. In the case of hydraulic (oil) damping, the fluid is forced through narrow openings or valves by one or more pistons.
- **DUAL-CLAMP:** Suspension fork with clamps that hold the stanchion tubes to the central steerer tube both above and below the bike's head tube. Used for forks with long travel and greater rigidity, specifically on freeride and downhill bikes.
- **COMPRESSION STAGE DAMPING:** The damping when the wheel is being forced up by an obstacle.
- **ECC:** Extension Control Cartridge, Marzocchi's name for their lock-out system.
- **ELASTOMER:** Plastic bumper or pad with little inherent damping.
- **HEADSHOK:** Suspension system built into the head tube rather than the fork. Based on the Browning patent, its primary user has been Cannondale.
- **LINKAGE FORK:** Suspension fork with rigid fork blades on which the suspension is achieved with a sprung parallelogram linkage.
- **MCU:** Micro-Cellular Urethane, an elastomer suitable as a spring element.
- **PURE DAMPING:** That's what Rock Shox calls its twin piston design.
- **QR 20:** A (hollow) oversize quick-release skewer of 20 mm diameter used by Marzocchi for their type 21 fork, which requires a special QR 20 hub.
- **RA:** Reverse Action technology used on some Manitou forks since the 2002 model year, on which the brake brace is mounted behind the fork rather than in front.
- **REBOUND DAMPING:** Damping during the return phase after the initial reaction.
- **RTA:** Rapid Travel Adjust, a method used by Manitou to adjust travel.
- **RESPONSIVENESS,** or **RESPONSE RATE:** Reaction of the suspension to a jolt. (see also STICTION)
- **SAG:** Negative spring travel, the amount of suspension travel taken up when the bike is loaded but no external force is applied. Depends on the rider's weight.
- **SHOCKBOOTS:** Neoprene sleeves to cover the exposed areas of the stanchion tubes, often only around the lower portion, to keep dirt and moisture out of the system.
- **SLIDERS:** The (usually) lower tubes of the fork, of larger diameter, into which the stanchion tubes slide.
- **STANCHIONS:** The (usually) upper tubes of the fork, of smaller diameter, which slide up and down in the slider tubes.
- **SPRING RESPONSE RATE:** Measure of relative spring resistance, quoted in lbs./in. (or sometimes in N/mm, where N stands for Newton, the scientific unit of force).
- **STICTION:** The force that has to be applied before the suspension reacts. If it is high, there is no discernable dive associated with e.g. pedaling while out of the seat. If it is low, the suspension reacts even to slight ripples in the surface.
- **TORSIONAL STIFFNESS:** The amount of force needed to divert the fork, and with it the front wheel, from the straight course, measured in Nm/degree.
- **TRAVEL:** The distance by which the front and/or rear wheel can move up or down. In the case of a suspension fork, the distance by which the stanchion tube moves into the slider tube.
- **TRIPLE CLAMP:** The equivalent of a fork crown on a telescoping suspension fork, clamping the two stanchion tubes to the steerer tube.
- **TULLIO:** Rock Shox through-axle design combining quick-release and bolted axle, used to increase front wheel and fork rigidity.
- **UPSIDE-DOWN:** Suspension fork on which the large-diameter slider tubes are at the top and the smaller-diameter stanchion tubes are at the bottom.
- **U-TURN:** Rock-Shox's adjustment system to adjust the amount of travel of the fork.
- **VARI-TRAVEL:** Infinitely variable suspension travel adjustment used on some Rock Shox forks.

for sale at drastically reduced prices. Often these one- or two-year-old models differ in no more than the color scheme from the current year's models. It's hard to tell just how much money you should spend on a suspension fork—and they can be had at prices ranging from under $100 to well over $1,000—but we definitely warn you to stay away from the cheapest models, because those are really only designed for street use, rather than serious off-road work.

Once you get to suspension forks with a nominal retail price between $300 and $500 (remember, that's not what you'll have to "fork out" if you mail order last year's model), you can expect to have pretty sophisticated adjustment possibilities for fine-tuning the riding characteristics, without sacrificing lateral rigidity or paying a weight penalty. Once you reach nominal prices of $600 and above, the improvements become pretty insignificant, expressed in terms of cost/benefit, unless you'll be participating in downhill competition riding.

Even if you have an older suspension fork on your bike, providing it's not damaged, you can probably keep up with the stormy development over the last decade. Most good forks sold since 1994 can be upgraded by replacing the internals by more modern ones from the same manufacturer. But before you spend good money to do that, check those ads to find out whether you cannot replace the entire fork for an upgraded model more cheaply.

Parallelogram linkage suspension fork with central hydraulic shock unit.

Cannondale's proprietary "Headshok" design, with a single spring element built around the fork's steerer tube.

More rigid, but also heavier: double crown fork for down-hill use.

HOW TO FIND A FITTING FORK FOR YOUR BIKE

Before you run out to buy a new suspension fork, it's important to make sure it will fit your bike. That's because you should not change the bike's geometry too much with the new fork, lest your nimble bike is lamed by unintentional changes that are due to the fact that the bike's front end is raised further off the ground and/or the front wheel is pulled back relative to the steering axis. After all, you're trying to improve, not jeopardize the bike's riding qualities.

The standard length of the old rigid fork was 395 mm (15½ in.), and every mountain bike frame in those days was designed for that length. Suspension forks, on the other hand, are longer because you have to add the distance of fork travel so the fork doesn't "bottom out" (i.e. the bottom of the fork crown hitting the top of the front tire, which would stop the front wheel dead in its track, catapulting the rider over the front). For this reason, modern frames are designed with the appropriate fork length in mind. If you put a suspension fork on a frame that was designed for a 395 mm rigid fork, it'll be raised off the ground further in the front. The effect will be that the steerer tube angle will be reduced (more "laid back"), which makes the bike's steering significantly less

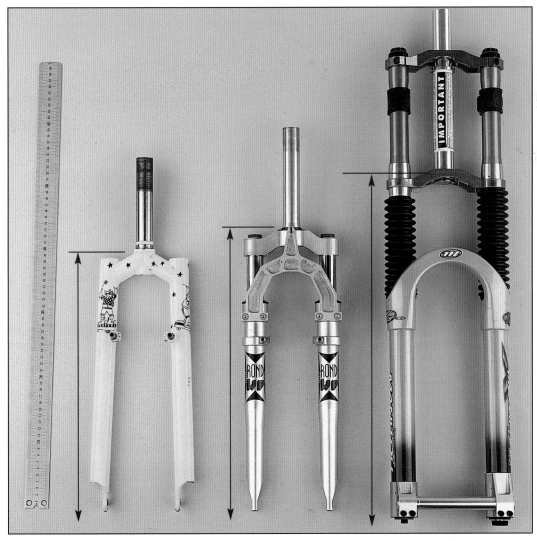

Whereas the rigid fork usually has an installed height of 395 mm (15½ in.), suspension forks can be anything up to 510 mm. Replacement forks must be selected to fit within the range of length that does not alter the bike's steering geometry too drastically.

53

agile. Even half a degree of difference has a negative effect on the steering. If the suspension fork is only 20 mm longer than the original fork, the effect is about one degree less steerer tube angle, and if you consider that a fork with 70 mm travel is 430 mm high (measured between the lower headset bearing and the center of the wheel axle), the difference is about 1.2 degrees under load if the fork is properly adjusted.

Now let's look at the effect of changes to the steerer tube angle. During the short but stormy development years of the mountain bike from converted clunker to hight-tech full-suspension technology, one standard has emerged for the steerer tube angle: between 70 and 71.5 degrees. If the angle is less ("shallower"), the

This "upside-down" suspension fork from the Italian suspension manufacturer Marzocchi has up to 190 mm (7½ in.) of travel, making it suitable for hardcore freeride and downhill use.

bike's steering becomes sluggish, whereas steerer tube angles of 72 degrees or more make the bike excessively "agile," or "nervous," depending on your point of view—or your level of skill, because too agile means you're always at work trying to keep the bike going where you want it to go.

So before you buy a suspension fork for your bike—regardless whether as a replacement for the one that's already there or to replace a rigid fork—you should first check the existing steerer tube angle. You can either find this out by asking the dealer or by looking it up in the manufacturer's catalogue, whether in print or on the Web. As an alternative, you can measure it yourself with the aid of a protractor and a plumb bob or a level gauge. There are even devices on the market that allow you to measure it directly.

Next you'll have to determine the nominal length of your bike's existing fork. Measure it from the center of the wheel hub to the bottom of the lower headset bearing. If the frame was designed with a suspension fork in mind, it will be more than the old standard length of 395 mm (15½ in.).

Now, as long as the new suspension fork does not exceed the length of the old fork by more than about 20 mm (¾ in.), you

can be reasonably sure your bike will still handle OK with the new fork, especially if your steerer tube angle did not exceed 71 degrees. If the steerer tube angle is 71½ degrees or more, you should not use a replacement fork that's more than 12 mm (½ in.) longer than the old one. And if your steerer tube angle is on the low side, like 70½ degrees, you can probably handle a fork that's up to 40 mm (1½ in.) longer than the old one.

Don't forget to measure the length of the existing fork before choosing a replacement suspension fork. Unless you know what that dimension is, you can't determine which suspension forks are suitable for use with your bike and which would be too long.

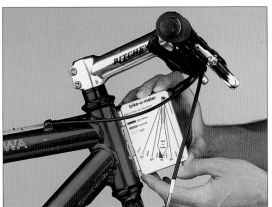

This simple cardboard "Bike-O-Meter" can be used to measure the angle of your steerer tube, also referred to as head tube angle (the head tube is part of the frame, while the steerer tube sits inside it as part of the fork).

Be warned, however, that the fork's installation length is not always proportional to the amount of travel of the fork: Choosing a longer fork does not necessarily mean you get that much more fork travel. First establish how much more fork length you can handle, then choose a fork with as much travel as you want that fits within that amount of extra length. To give an example, a 1999 Manitou Spider has 70 mm of travel and has the same length as a 1999 Rock Shox Judy, which has only 63 mm of travel. And even that does not mean that the Spider would be better than the Judy, because travel is not the only thing that matters, and factors such as response rate, damping, bottom-out cushioning, etc. are also important. Read the reviews in the mountain biking magazines and/or ask the dealer to make sure you get the most suitable fork for your situation.

So far we've only talked about the fork's installed length, but of course the steerer tube (i.e. the single tube at the top of the fork also matters. Make sure it is cut off at the right length for your bike's head tube plus the headset's "stacking height" (that's the sum of the height of all the components of the headset as far as they are not hidden inside the bike's head tube, a dimension that is given in the headset manufacturer's catalogue).

U-Turn is what Rock Shox calls this adjustment mechanism for the range of travel. The length of the spring inside the fork leg can be varied by turning the knob on top of the stanchion. Depending on the model in question, this allows for adjusting the amount of travel between 60 mm and 100 mm. The U-Turn system has been used on the Rock Shox Psylo model since 2002.

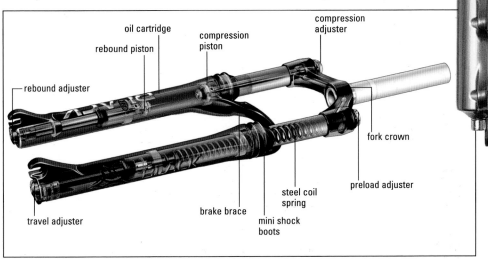

oil cartridge

rebound piston

compression piston

compression adjuster

rebound adjuster

fork crown

travel adjuster

brake brace

steel coil spring

mini shock boots

preload adjuster

The guts of a Manitou suspension fork exposed. This is a model on which travel and compression and rebound can all be adjusted. Like most modern forks of the mid- to high-end price range, it works with steel coil springs for suspension and an oil reservoir for damping.

8 SUSPENSION FORK MAINTENANCE

Don't chuck your old suspension fork when it's not performing quite up to par. On the following pages, you'll find specific maintenance and upgrading advice for the most common high-quality forks on the market today.

ROCK SHOX PSYLO MAINTENANCE

The Psylo is Rock Shox's top model. It offers adjustable travel, several different force ratings, adjustable compression and rebound, oil-tuning, and adjustable preload. As long as you take the trouble to adjust and maintain it, this is one of the finest forks around.

1 DAILY MAINTENANCE

After every ride, wash and then dry the fork, wiping away from the seals. Then apply some lubricant to the seals and compress the fork by 1 to 2 cm (⅜ to ¾ in.). That keeps them supple and responsive, minimizing initial "sticktion" (that's suspension terminology for the fork's initial resistance to movement—see the box "Suspension Glossary" on page 51). Just like the chain, the front fork's seals should be cared for after every ride. Use a low-viscosity oil, such as Brunox Rock Shox Deo, which prevents the adhesion of dirt.

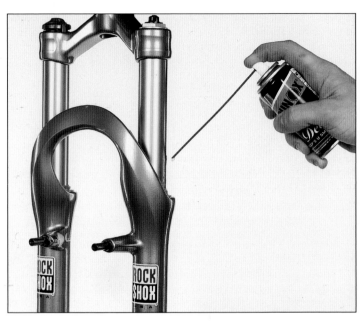

2 MONTHLY MAINTENANCE

After about 25 hours of riding, Rock Shox recommends you treat your fork to a tune-up. Inspect it carefully, also checking the condition of the neoprene seals between the stanchions and the sliders. Replace any seals on which the material is damaged or cracked.

In order to take a look behind the scenes for a more thorough inspection, you should occasionally partially disassemble the fork. Place the bike upside down, then pull the rebound adjuster knob off. Loosen the bolts at the ends of the fork but don't remove them completely. Now remove the tubes by hitting them on the head with the rubber mallet, while holding them with one hand. Then remove the bolts and pull the stanchions out.

Using a screwdriver with a cloth wrapped around it, lift the seals off; then clean and inspect their condition. Replace them if they show any damage, and lubricate them (e.g. with Rock Shox RedRum), then reassemble in reverse order.

3 CLEANING THE INSIDE

At least once a season— once every 50 hours of use according to the manufacturer—the fork needs to be completely overhauled. This tune-up comprises flushing the entire system, followed by repacking all of the moving parts with grease, and an oil change. Unless you're technically well-versed, this is the kind of job we recommend you leave to the bike shop. If you do want to take on this project yourself, you first have to remove the fork from the bike.

PSYLO TUNING

The following steps, continuing from the preceding ones, show you how to get the most out of your Psylo suspension fork if you're ready to take on that job yourself.

4 TRAVEL

Psylo XC and SL of the first generation work with what the manufacturer calls the "Varitravel" system: Turn the spring preload knob back all the way. Now remove the left-hand (looking from behind) stanchion cover plate using a 24 mm box wrench (to our British readers, that's what Americans call a ring spanner). Remove the spring. Adjust the screw inside the stanchion tube with a long screwdriver (the blade must be at least 22 cm, or 9 in., long. Turn the screwdriver clockwise to achieve less travel (and increased preload), to the right for more travel (and decreased preload).

On the Psylo Race, travel is adjusted by means of spacers (All Travel 80/100/125 mm) This is how it's done: Release the air out of both chambers. Remove the stanchions from the sliders (see facing page). Unscrew the left cover plate. Remove the circlip from the bottom of the slider and carefully pull the air piston rod. Replace any lubricant that gets lost in this process upon completion of the job. Install or remove spacers on the piston rod as required for the amount of travel you want. The fewer spacers, the more travel.

5 SPRING TENSION

Rock Shox offers eight different springs for the SL/XC to match rider weights from 35 to 135 kg (75 to 300 lbs). The Psylo Race uses air as a suspension spring, so all you have to do there is to adjust the air pressure. For a rider weight between 65 and 85 kg (140 and 185 lbs respectively), the recommended pressure range is between 100 and 140 PSI (7 and 10 bar respectively), and some trial and error will tell you what's best for your use.

The response rate is adjusted by means of "negative" air pressure (the air in the lower part of the system, beneath the piston). If the negative air pressure is only a little less than the compression air pressure, the fork is extremely soft, reacting immediately to any bumps. However, there's a downside: too much negative air pressure pulls the fork in and so reduces the amount of available travel.

6 SPRING TENSION

On the SL and Race models, damping can be adjusted by means of the Climb-it Control.

For all other models (but also for these two), damping characteristics can be tuned by selecting an oil with higher or lower viscosity (the more viscous, the more damping). Viscosity of oils change from their rated values depending on temperature. Ex-works, they are supplied with an oil rated 5W. If you often use the bike at low temperatures, you can try an even lower viscosity, whereas you may try oil with a higher viscosity if you frequently ride at high temperatures.

U-TURN RETROFIT

If you want to upgrade an older Psylo XC, SL, or C (pre-2002), you can install the U-Turn with the aid of an aftermarket kit. This system allows you to reduce the amount of travel when going uphill. Although the manual that comes with the kit describes the installation process, it's quite tricky, and consequently Rock Shox recommends having that job done by a bike mechanic.

TIPS & TRICKS

- To help lubricate the upper part of the fork, you can store your bike upside down overnight.
- Hold the fork upside-down when cleaning the stanchion tubes, which will prevent dirt from entering the fork.
- Materials for changing the damping oil of your fork can be bought at a drugstore (chemist in Britain): measuring cup, large syringe, etc.
- Instead of buying the fork manufacturer's product, you can use the equivalent product sold for cars (ATF oil), which is much cheaper. Just make sure it's the right viscosity.
- When washing the bike, don't aim a direct spray of water at the fork seals. One way of protecting them is by tying a piece of cloth around them.

ROCK SHOX SID

SID suspension forks are a joy to ride in rough terrain. However, they are trickier than other models when it comes to adjusting and maintenance. Here's what you need to know in order to handle this work with confidence.

1 DAILY MAINTENANCE

First remove (i.e. unscrew) the top caps from the top of the stanchion tubes (see photo) and pressurize the air chambers to the right pressure in accordance with the table below. Quickly unscrew the pump to avoid losing air in the process. Then install the top caps again.

2 FINE-TUNING

Tie a ziptie around one of the stanchion tubes, as shown in the photo, and push it all the way down against the top of the slider. Now get on the bike and check how far the ziptie rides up on the stanchion, which corresponds to the amount of negative travel. For racing use, it should go about 10 percent of the total travel, for others it should be about 20 percent.

If it's not even close, you should correct the air pressure. Leave the ziptie in place so you can check the results of reinflating the upper and lower air chambers (step 3).

Recommended Air Pressure

Rider weight	Pressure
less than 100 lbs. (55 kg)	30–40 PSI (2.1–2.8 bar)
100–115 lbs. (55–64 kg)	40–50 PSI (2.8–3.5 bar)
115–130 lbs. (64–73 kg)	50–60 PSI (3.5–4.1 bar)
130–150 lbs. (73–82 kg)	55–65 PSI (3.8–.4.5 bar)
more than 115 lbs. (82 kg)	65–75 PSI (4.5–5.2 bar)

Maximum allowable pressure: 100 PSI (6.9 bar)

3 NEGATIVE AIR PRESSURE

Dual Air (SID Race, SL, XL)

For racing use, pressurize the negative air chamber to 50-70 percent of the positive air pressure, for other uses, 70 to 100 percent. Remember that the negative air pressure influences the suspension characteristics over the first third of travel. So check whether the fork is now collapsed further when you sit on the bike and if necessary repeat steps 2 and 3.

Hydra Air (SID 100, XC)

In these models, the negative function is provided by a coil spring, installed in the bottom of the left-hand slider, and consequently you can't adjust it. This is really a modified version of the Hydra-Air technology Rock Shox used on the first generation of SID forks.

4
DAMPING ADJUSTMENT

In the case of the Hydra-Air models, the rebound stage is adjusted together with the compression stage damping by means of the adjusting screw at the bottom of the right-hand dropout. Turn it clockwise to increase damping, counterclockwise to reduce it.

Dual-Air forks have separate adjusters for the compression and rebound damping. When the adjusting screw is in its normal position, it adjusts the rebound damping, while it adjusts compression stage damping when it is pulled out.

Reminder: Compression stage damping prevents "bottoming out," while rebound damping helps reduce "bounciness" of the front end of the bike.

RECOMMENDED DAMPING OIL LEVELS
If you like it light, you can't go far wrong with a SID fork

Model	Travel	Use	Weight*
DUAL AIR			
SID Race	63 mm	CC Race	1,156 g
SID SL	63/80 mm	CC & Marathon	1,230 g
SID XL	80/100 mm	Full Susp. & Freeride	1,745 g
HYDRA-AIR			
SID 100	100 mm	Marathon & Full Susp.	1,497 g
SID XC	63/80 mm	CC & Marathon	1,380 g

* Per author's measurements

MAINTENANCE TIPS

- Clean the stanchion tubes and the dampers after every off-road ride, and then spray some penetrating oil, such as Brunox on the tubes.

- Occasionally place the bike upside down for some time to allow the oil from the bottom of the sliders to reach all the way up to the seals and bushings.

- Remove the dampers after about 20 to 30 hours of off-road use and lubricate the attachment points with bearing grease.

- If the unit gradually loses air pressure, don't be concerned that it necessarily

means the seals are shot: check the valves of the air chambers and occasionally replace them. You can buy cheap replacement valves and the appropriate tools in any automobile parts store.

- In case you have problems with the Rock Shox pump, we suggest you try

the DMM pump (also known as "Flamethrower"), on which air does not escape when connecting and disconnecting it to the valve.

- Due to the complicated design of the SID suspension elements, there's only a small number of maintenance jobs you can carry out.

MARZOCCHI MAINTENANCE

Here's how you can increase the amount of travel on Marzocchi Bomber forks starting with the 2000 model year. There are four models on which you can vary the amount of travel for 100 or 130 mm.

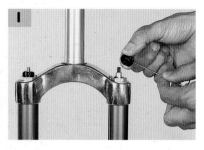

1
OPENING THE TOP CAPS

The Marzocchi Bomber models on which the amount of travel can be upgraded from 100 to 130 mm are the Z 1 MCR (used in the illustrations as an example), as well as the Z 1 CR, Z 1 QR 20, and Z 1 QR 20 models. The upgrade kit consists of two longer main springs and two shorter rebound springs. Before you start, completely release the preload tension of the springs by twisting them counterclockwise. First remove the preload adjusting knobs using a 1.5 mm Allen wrench (Fig. 1). Next, carefully pry out the circlip from the opening using a narrow screwdriver (Fig. 3). Before you open the cap, make sure the fork is upright, to prevent oil from escaping. In the case of MCR model forks, the cap can be removed with a 21 mm open-ended wrench (Fig. 3). For other models, the stanchions must first be pulled out of the fork crown before you can remove the cap (Note: First remove the additional clip). Once the cap has been removed, the spring preload adjustment nut is exposed. Careful: These nuts have left-hand screw thread, so they must be turned clockwise to remove, counterclockwise to reinstall. (Fig. 4). Compressing the fork a little will improve access.

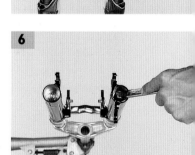

2
SPRING REMOVAL

Now the main springs can be pulled out (5). Note that the lower portion of the spring is color-coded to identify its tension. Also note that the white plastic ring on the spring is installed with the recess facing up.

Up to this point, the procedure is the same as for replacing the springs by harder or softer versions. If you're going to increase the amount of travel, this is the time to pour the oil out from the top of the sliders. Unless you can reuse the oil, please dispose of it in a responsible manner by taking it for recycling. Move the piston rod up and down to help drain the last drops of fluid.

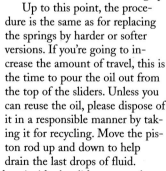

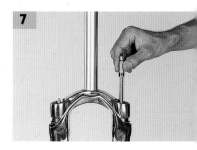

The rebound springs, which lie deep inside the sliders, must also be removed when you upgrade the travel. They can be accessed once you have removed the damping units in both legs. The locknuts for the damping units are somewhat recessed at the bottom of the sliders. You'll need a long 15 mm open-ended wrench (Fig. 6). If the damping units rotate with the nuts, you can pull them out up to the stop at the top and hold them firmly. (Fig. 7)

Versatility is tops with the Marzocchi Bomber Z1. On account of its adjustable travel, it's suitable for almost any terrain.

3
REMOVAL OF DAMPING UNIT

After the lower installation nuts have been removed, you can pull the damper units out from the top (Fig. 8). Originally, the compression stage damping is in the right-hand slider tube as seen from the front, while the rebound damping is in the left-hand slider. They're marked with a slotted black and silver adjusting knob respectively. Theoretically, you can reverse their position, however, once you get used to their location, you don't want to change that. Out on the trail, you'll be more likely to want to adjust the compression damping, and that's then most conveniently reached with the right hand from the rider position on the bike.

The easiest way to replace the rebound springs is with the aid of a spoke: Hold the spoke from the threaded end and use the head as a hook to pull the spring from the slider (Fig. 9). In order to upgrade to the long travel kit, you replace the original long rebound spring with the new shorter one from the kit (Fig. 10).

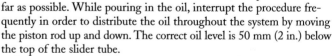

4
OIL CHANGE

Reassemble the fork in reverse sequence. Before you install the main spring (as described in step 5, below), the damping oil must be replaced (Fig. 11). To do this, compress the fork as far as possible. While pouring in the oil, interrupt the procedure frequently in order to distribute the oil throughout the system by moving the piston rod up and down. The correct oil level is 50 mm (2 in.) below the top of the slider tube.

A convenient way to do this is with a large syringe from the drugstore, placing a 2-inch long piece of tubing over the nozzle, and then using the syringe to suck out any excess oil from the top (Fig. 12).

Damping Tuning: The fork's damping characteristics can be varied slightly by adjusting the oil level. If you fill in 2 to 3 mm more oil (0.08-0.125 in.), reduce the damping. Another way to adjust the damping is by choosing an oil with higher viscosity (W10 or W 15). However, experience with these systems suggests that the adjustability of the damping is big enough to manage well with the standard W 7.5 oil that Marzocchi recommends.

A complete oil change is usually required only once every two years, but you may want to do it annually if you ride a lot.

MANITOU MAINTENANCE

Answer Products' Manitou forks are built in such a way that the average mountain biker can handle their maintenance and adjustment operations without fear. These suspension forks require neither special tools nor mechanical expertise. Your most important "special" tool will be a grease gun.

MICROLUBE FOR EASY LUBRICATION

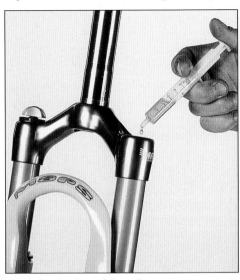

Manitou has developed something they refer to as Microlube to simplify the lubrication of the slider tubes. Using a grease gun, simply squeeze two or three shots of lubricant in the grease nipples of the sliders, which will keep them operating smoothly for 100 hours of riding (several months' worth for most riders). Do this more frequently if you do a lot of downhill riding in very rough terrain—up to once every 20 hours of operation. And if you have completely disassembled and cleaned your fork, 20 squirts of the grease gun is all it takes to get it back to work.

The Manitou models that work with compressed air as the suspension medium, such as the Mars series, need a little more care once every 100 to 200 hours of operation. After releasing all the air from the air chamber, you should lubricate the air piston (if you forget to release the air pressure, you risk having the cover cap shoot out at you). In order to do this, first remove the end cap on the left side (as seen from the rider's position on the bike), using a 27 mm box wrench—it doesn't fit very well, but for reasons known only to the designer, and perhaps not even to him or her, there is neither a metric nor a standard size wrench that fits the odd size cap they put on there. Squirt some fork oil in the opening and close the cap again.

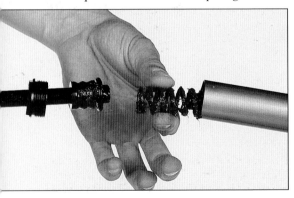

If the fork often bottoms out or hardly seems to respond at all, it's usually due to the wrong selection of springs for the rider weight. Also check the air pressure and the oil level and adjust them accurately.

COIL SPRINGS

For the Mars series, Manitou makes four different spring tensions. In order to replace the springs, you first have to remove both the stanchions and the sliders. This is how you go about it: Remove the rebound adjuster knob from the bottom of the right-hand slider by simply pulling it off (in the case of the Mars Elite model). Loosen the 8 mm Allen bolt from the right-hand slider, the 4 mm Allen bolt from the left-hand slider, and then pull the sliders down off the stanchions. Loosen the plastic bolt that is now exposed in the left slider, using a 24 mm open-ended wrench, and pull out the compression rod. Pull the spring out with your little finger. Now you can install the new spring after lubricating it generously with thick bearing grease.

In the case of the X-Vert, SX, and Magnum models, the springs are exchanged from the top instead of from the bottom. Simply remove the end cap on the left side (as seen from the rider's position on the bike) and remove the elastomer pads with the spring. The new springs are always supplied complete with the matching elastomer pads. Lubricate with thick grease and reinstall.

RIDER WEIGHT RATINGS

Here's a summary of the available Manitou springs and the rider weight for which they are designed. They retail at about $20 a set.

Color code	Spring rating		Corresponding air pressure for the Mars model
Blue	below 110 lbs (52 kg)		approx. 5.5 bar (80 psi)
Red	110-175 lbs (52-79 kg)		6.6-8.6 bar (100-125 psi)
Yellow	175-220 lbs (79-104 kg)		9.4-11.3 bar (240-165 psi)
Black	over 220 lbs (104 kg)		up to approx. 13 bar (190 psi)

> Oil levels in mm for 2001 and later models:
> Magnum R: 107 mm ▪ SX/SX-100/SX R: 108 mm ▪ Mars/Mars Elite/ Mars Super: 114/102/95 mm ▪ X-Vert/X-Vert Super/X-Vert Air: 79 mm ▪ X-Vert DC/X-Vert Carbon: 254/215 mm ▪ Super Nova: 114 mm/minus 5 mm. For forks equipped with the Anti-BOB system the exact dimensions must be maintained. For other models, deviations of several mm are OK.

OIL CHANGE MADE EASY

Removing the fork from the bike makes it easier to drain the oil. Open the right-hand stanchion tube (as seen from the rider's position on the bike), using a 24 mm open-ended wrench. Pour the oil out and dispose of it by taking it to a recycling station. It's recommended to release the air pressure from the left fork tube, which makes it easy to move the fork in and out a few times in order to help push the last drop of oil out.

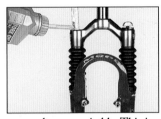

REPLACING THE OIL

You can use any kind of AT oil in the viscosity range from 2.5 W (for minimal damping) to 10 W (for maximum damping). The multi-viscosity Motorex oil has proven to be very suitable. This is an oil with a viscosity range that adjusts itself to the ambient temperature: It gets thinner in cold weather and thicker in warm weather within the range from 5 to 10 W. Pour the fresh oil in and check the level difference between the top of the oil and the top of the fork crown with a measuring rod, with the fork fully extended. The oil levels are listed in the box above. This operation should be carried out after a minimum of 100 hours of use but at least once every 2 years.

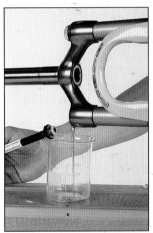

This is what you need to upgrade your SX-R or Mars suspension fork: Manitou's Anti-BOB lockout system can be retrofitted on these forks. But make sure the oil level is correct.

REPLACING THE OIL

The forks of the types Magnum R, SX 100, and Mars are often characterized by excessive damping, meaning their response to an obstacle is too slow for most riders' tastes. That can easily be corrected. In order to do that, remove the damping piston rod from the right-hand fork leg. Enlarge the oil flow ports in the lower plate with the help of a 2 mm drill bit and an electric drill. If it's still too slow for your liking, you can increase their diameter to 2.5 mm, or by drilling one or two additional 2 mm holes. Reinstall and test operation after every change to make sure you don't accidentally eliminate the desired damping effect. The fork's warranty should remain valid despite this change.

IMPORTANT NOTE: All the bolts on Manitou forks should only be tightened to 3-5 Nm (2-3.5 ftlb). You don't need any noticeable force to reach this amount of torque. (Nm, or Newton-meter, and ftlb, or footpound, are measures of torque or moment, and to play it safe, you should use a torque wrench to match these values.)

HEADSHOK MAINTENANCE

Excellent functionality and optimal response rate. With regular maintenance, you can get the most out of your Cannondale Headshok suspension system.

The Cannondale Headshok suspension system lies elegantly hidden—and protected—inside the head tube. Even so, you'll only get the best performance out of this system if you take the trouble to maintain it regularly. Here we'll use the Fatty D as an example to show you which essential maintenance operations you can easily carry out

yourself. Even changing the oil on this most popular of the Headshok versions is not beyond the ability of most competent biker-mechanics. This operation does require the use of Cannondale-specific tools, as illustrated on the facing page.

On the Fatty D, a steel coil spring with internal elastomer pads is responsible for the suspen-

sion function, while damping is taken care of by an oil system. The following description of the basic maintenance inspection is equally applicable to other Headshok models, such as the Fatty SL, P-Bone D, and P-Bone M. In each case, it is important to observe that the suspension must be in non-locked-out position.

BASIC MAINTENANCE CHECK

Operation should be checked after every serious downhill ride, regardless of which Headshok model is installed on your bike.

2. Lubricate the upper headset bearing with a common lubricant, such as chain lubricant, on a regular basis. Just apply a drop to both sides, while turning the bike's steering from left to right and back again. The lower bearing is well protected against the penetration of dirt and water inside the system. If your bike is equipped with the compressed-air-sprung Fatty SL system, the air pressure should be checked once every two weeks.

1. Check the neoprene bellows for cracks and tears. That's easiest to do if you pull the ends apart a little. Also check for proper seating of the cable attachments at the top and the bottom. If the material is damaged, it's best to replace it immediately, because if water is allowed to enter the bellows, it's likely to affect the needle bearings of the suspension, causing damage to that sensitive system.

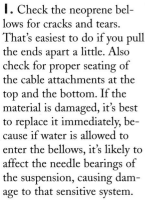

Headshok suspension units can be tuned by using different coil springs. And to carry out the oil change, you need the special Cannondale wrench depicted in the center of the illustration, in addition to the other standard tools shown.

MAJOR TUNE-UP

Once every 40 hours of operation, and at least after every ride in wet weather, the following operations should be carried out. The difference between the various Headshok models is only a matter of the installation of the adjusting knob.

1. First remove the black knob from the top of the stem. On the P-Bone D and Fatty D models, that's done with a 4 mm Allen wrench to remove the Allen bolt on top, while the knob on the Fatty SL is held with a 3 mm grub screw from the side; on the P-Bone M, the knob is merely clamped on and you can pull it off by hand.

Next remove the stem clamp by loosening the Allen bolt that clamps it around the fork's steerer tube. This is done in order to free the cartridge cover plate, and there's no need to remove the stem itself.

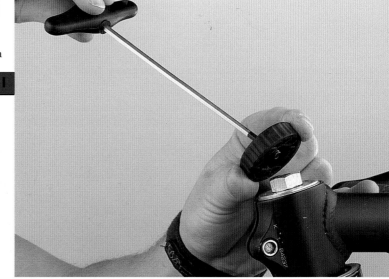

2. Now remove the cartridge cover plate with a pin wrench, such as the adjustable one from Park Tools by turning it counterclockwise. Whatever you do, don't try to remove it by unscrewing the 19 mm hexagonal bolt on top. Even after you've removed the cover, the cartridge itself is not exposed yet, so no oil will run out.

3. Remove the upper cable tie at the neoprene bellows and pull it down somewhat. Using the pin wrench, check the lower lockring to make sure it is tight, and tighten it first if necessary. (It must be tightly screwed into the head tube to prevent the fork from falling out once the cartridge has been removed.)

Don't attempt to disassemble the fork and its cartridge yourself because the needle bearings inside make it beyond the scope of what the home mechanic can safely do—leave that to a Cannondale-trained bike shop mechanic.

4. Now turn the bike upside-down. The four flattened surfaces of the fork's steerer tube can now easily be cleaned. Then coat these surfaces with thick oil and distribute it into the bearing by pushing the fork up-and-down. If lubricated with oil, as opposed to bearing grease, the suspension will remain responsive even in cold weather.

Attach the bellows with a new ziptie. Reinstall the cartridge cover plate; tighten the stem clamp bolt (while making sure the handlebars are straight with respect to the front wheel, which can be reinstalled before you do that); and reinstall the adjusting knob on top. That's all there is to it, and your Headshok fork is as good as new.

PARTS AND TOOLS

Headshok maintenance made easy: Use the tools depicted on page 67 for all the maintenance you'll ever want to do.

- Shock-Boot with zipties
- Fatty D seal set
- Cannondale fork oil W 5
- Coil springs/elastomer set for Fatty D, soft/medium/hard
- Cannondale "Castle Tool" for cartridge removal or installation
- Allen wrenches in sizes 3, 4, and 5 mm
- Park Tools pin wrench

Available from any Cannondale dealers

9 REAR SUSPENSION MAINTENANCE

You've barely started your ride and trouble starts on the first downhill: Oil gushes from the damper, and not a bike shop in sight. Your full-suspension bike becomes a pogo stick. Your case is not an exception, as we've found during our many years of test-riding full-suspension bikes of all types, makes, and models. In fact, poorly conceived designs, inadequate bearings, and leaky shocks can cause some bikes to be hypochondriacs, suffering one setback after another. That, unfortunately, has given full-suspension bikes a bad rap in some circles of the mountain biking community. However, there are easy ways of preventing most of these troubles, which will make biking the joy it should be in the first place.

Let's look at the bearings of pivot points first. Their quality can be anything from poor to excellent. Coated pivot bushings are particularly sensitive to abuse. Just pushing in the bearing pin a little too forcefully can damage the coating, and the damage will quickly spread with use.

As for lubrication, if you think a little is good, so more must be better, you're on the wrong track: Excessive lubrication often promotes dirt particles settling on and around the bearings and finally penetrate within. In fact, many types of journal bearings should not be lubricated at all—don't overdo it, and check the manual to make sure you're lubricating only in places where lubrication is recommended, using only the specific lubricants suggested.

If the bearing is clearly deteriorating, the question arises whether to fix it yourself or take it to the bike shop for repair. Warning: If you don't have the appropriate tools for the job, you're likely to do more damage just taking things apart and putting them back together again. So decide whether you have the

If the shock unit leaks and the linkages squeal, it's time to take your full-suspension bike for intensive care. With the minor surgery operations described in the following pages, it will be back on its feet in no time.

exact tools recommended in the manual for the job at hand and whether it's worth purchasing them yourself. In our opinion it's well worth the investment in tools to be able to work on your full-suspension bike yourself with confidence. Buy those tools before you start.

Many pivot bearing problems can be prevented by assuring they receive the regular maintenance that's specific to their type (see the box on this page). The job is easiest on bikes with maintenance-free bearings. This category includes both pre-lubricated sealed ball or roller bearings and self-lubricating journal bearings. However, even having bearings of one of those types does not mean you should be encouraged to just let your bike take care of itself: At some point, even a supposedly maintenance-free bearing is near the end of its life and needs to be replaced. When that is, depends on the quality of the bearing and the seals, as well as the maintenance the bike receives. For instance, if you don't bother to keep the seals clean and check their position from time to time, dirt may enter and ruin the bearing pretty quickly.

Use special bearing lubricant for sealed main pivot bearings to maximize their useful life.

Sure, it would be nice to have a full-suspension bike that really doesn't need any maintenance at all, and you may be tempted to think that's what you've got when you buy one with "maintenance-free" bearings. It could probably be done—if you don't mind a bike that weighs a ton and costs one

too. That's why most manufacturers recommend something on the lines of: "Although our rear tri-angle is equipped with mainte-nance-free

Sealed ball or roller bearing units in the main pivots present few problems.

pivot bearings, we recommend regular check-ups."

So now for those regular check-ups, the easiest way and time to do that is in conjunction with regular cleaning of the bike. As you're washing and wiping the bike, check out all the sensitive points to make sure the seals are still intact and the pivots don't ei-

ther have too much play or are too tight, with "rough spots" in their range of movement. Also pay attention as you ride the bike, and thoroughly inspect any part that makes uncalled-for noise. When cleaning the bike after each ride in the dirt, wash and wipe away from the pivots and seals to prevent water and/or dirt from entering those parts. Check and correct anything you find: loose bolts or nuts, bent pieces, cracked or partially unseated seals, etc.

From time to time, it's not a bad idea to remove the rear shock unit completely after you finish cleaning the bike. This will allow you to move the rear triangle over its entire range. If something is loose or otherwise amiss, you're much more likely to identify it

PIVOT BEARING MAINTENANCE

Not all full-suspension pivot bearings are identical, and each type needs its own specific type of maintenance.

SEALED ROLLER BEARING UNITS
Roller bearings with seal covers on both sides are lubricated for life and are consequently referred to as maintenance free and very resistant to moisture and dirt penetration. Lubrication is not necessary. If they do fail, you can easily replace the entire unit as one piece. Make sure you get units with lip-seals, which are well sealed on both sides and can be recognized by the code 2RS in their type designation.

OPEN ROLLER BEARINGS
Unlike sealed roller bearings, open roller bearings can be taken apart. They're rarely used on mountain bikes these days. Once you disassemble them, they are easy to clean, inspect, and lubricate. Use only special bearing grease. Although they can be disassembled, they should still be protected with flexible seals on both sides, and these seals should be carefully removed, inspected, and reinstalled—and replaced if damaged. They can be just as well-protected against the penetration of dirt and moisture, and they can be just as easily replaced as sealed bearings.

SELF-LUBRICATING BEARINGS
These are journal bearings (i.e. without intermediate balls or rollers between the two bearing surfaces) with bearing surfaces that are specially coated (with e.g. Teflon) instead of conventional lubricants. You don't need to lubricate them because the addition of greasy lubricants only acts to attract and enter dirt particles inside the bearings. That would quickly ruin the special coating and bind up the bearing. Once they are worn, they require complete replacement, including the bearing spindle, which in effect is part of the bearing unit. Because of the extremely sensitive coating, you should never approach these bearings without special tools.

CONVENTIONAL JOURNAL BEARINGS
These consist of bearing bushings (or pivot bushings) and bearing pins. Unlike their self-lubricating counterparts, they require generous lubrication of the bearing surfaces. All you can do is disassemble, clean, inspect, lubricate, and reassemble them. If they can't be made to work quietly, without high resistance or looseness, it's time to replace at least the bushings, sometimes also the pins. Take care to use the correct type of lubricant, because using conventional grease on models with nylon or other plastic bushings will quickly ruin them. Special tools are usually required to remove and reinstall them. They should also be protected with some kind of external seal, for which you can use a glob of grease on models with metal bushings (only).

this way than when you're working against the resistance of the shock unit. How often you do that depends on the kind of use the bike gets. If you live in an area with wet and muddy terrain, you'll need to do that more frequently than if

you live in a mild climate with little

Right: Coil-spring shock unit.
Left: Air-sprung shock unit

rain. For wet-weather riding, we recommend installing some kind of fender—the kind that just clips on the bike. As an alternate, you can push an old rubber inner tube of adequate size over the outside of the shock unit to protect it, as long as you make sure it doesn't interfere with the shock's operation.

It's certainly time for a serious overhaul/replacement when the shock unit noticeably stops working properly, when oil spray emanates from it during the ride, or when you find oil dribbling down along the outside: These are signs that the seals are shot, usually caused by the penetration of dirt and water into the seals, causing excessive wear.

A second cause for this problem can be the application of excessive bending forces on the piston rod. And that's usually caused by the shock unit being clamped in without adequate freedom of movement due to a stuck pivot, either at the top or the bottom. In that case, there's nothing you can do except replace the unit and take care not to let that happen again by way of frequent inspection.

We suggest you don't try to disassemble a leaky or otherwise defective shock unit yourself, unless you have access to the specific tools and follow the manufacturer's instructions given in the manual to the letter. The high gas pressure inside some models makes it quite dangerous to play around with them yourself. Damage to the shock unit pivot bearings, on the other hand, can easily be handled by the home mechanic. Usually these pivot points are held in place with small pivot bearing bushes that require the same kind of maintenance as those used for the rear triangle's other pivots. And here too, it's preventive maintenance that pays off: Regular cleaning and lubricating only as much as recommended by the manufacturer and with the lubricants specified (or without lubrication if that's what the manufacturer recommends) is all it takes. When cleaning these parts, just as with all other bearing points on the bike, you should not direct a strong water jet at them: Use a bucket with water and a sponge or a rag, replacing the water frequently so you're always working with clean water.

After you've finished cleaning, pay particular attention to the shock unit pivot points. These points must rotate freely, the shock unit following without any noticeable resistance or distortion. If you don't prevent this kind of problem, you're bound to have more serious breakdowns of the shock unit very soon.

The next item to check is the screw thread for the coil spring preload adjustment. Keep it clean and lightly lubricated in order to

prevent the binding of this screw thread, which would eliminate the adjustability feature and hinder removal or installation of the shock unit. The best type of lubricant for this purpose is a paraffin-based "dry" lubricant applied from a spray can. This kind of lubricant (also used for the chain and cables) does not attract dirt the way other lubricants do.

TIPS & TRICKS

ROLLER BEARINGS
- Sealed bearing units should only be cleaned externally, never with the use of a high-pressure jet.
- Frequently check the bearings to make sure they operate smoothly. Remove the shock unit to do this.
- If the bearing has a lubricating nipple, don't forget to lubricate it with a grease gun after every ride in wet weather or terrain.
- Only disassemble the bearings if there's a problem with them that can't be solved without disassembly.
- Be careful not to apply unequal force to the inner and outer bearing races.

JOURNAL BEARINGS
- Self-lubricating journal bearings should not be lubricated except as directed by the manufacturer, using only the recommended lubricants.
- Check and lubricate non-self-lubricating bearings at regular intervals.
- Frequently check the bearings for ease and smoothness of operation. To do that, first remove the shock unit.
- Regularly check the external seals to make sure they are seated properly.

SHOCK UNITS
- Regularly check their attachments to make sure they rotate freely.
- Make sure the shock unit is adjusted correctly for the rider's weight in accordance with the instruction manual.
- Use spring units that correspond to the rider's weight.
- Always keep the screw thread for preload adjustment clean.
- Check to make sure no frame parts can come in contact with the shock unit when the suspension is pushed in all the way.
- Use a protector over the shock unit in bad weather. But don't forget to keep things clean underneath.

TREK UNIFIED REAR TRIANGLE

On these pages you will find the jobs that are typically required on a bike with integrated rear triangle suspension, shown here on a Trek bike but also valid for other makes.

REAR TRIANGLE CHECK

The rear triangle unit should be checked once every six months or so to make sure it moves freely and without excessive looseness. It should also be done after any unusually demanding ride (higher than normal speeds, rougher terrain then normal, etc.). This is how you go about it.

Remove the rear wheel, then remove the rear bolt on the shock unit (i.e. the one that holds it to the rear triangle). It should be possible to rotate the rear triangle around the pivot point with just a little, constant resistance, and it should not be possible to move it sideways at all. The pivot bearing has to be overhauled if the movement is either too loose or not smooth, or the pivot bearing is noisy as you do this.

BEARING CHECK

First remove the right-hand crank, the chain, and any cables that run to the rear triangle (brake and gear cables). Remove the bolts at the sides of the main pivot point bearing, using two 6 mm Allen wrenches, after which you can pull out the pivot axle, which detaches the rear triangle from the main frame.

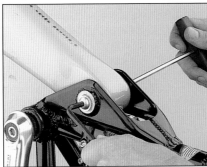

Clean all the pivot bearing parts thoroughly and inspect them for damage, replacing any parts that are damaged or worn. Since (at least on the Trek models) this is a self-lubricating bearing, you should not apply lubricant.

Apply Loctite Blue thread locking compound to the screw thread of the bolts so they don't come loose unexpectedly.

TECHNICAL DATA AND MAINTENANCE INTERVALS

- **REAR SUSPENSION TYPE:** Single pivot integrated rear triangle.
- **BEARING TYPE:** Teflon-coated journal bearing.
- **BEARING REPLACEMENT COST:** Around U.S. $25 per bushing set.
- **BEARING MAINTENANCE INTERVAL:** Once every 6 months or 2,000 km (1,250 miles), but immediately if any problems occur (e.g. play, noise, etc.).
- **SHOCK UNIT:** Fox Vanilla/Vanilla C (oil/air) for models Y 11, Y22, Y 33; Fox Vanilla X/Vanilla R/Vanilla RX (coils spring/ail) for models Y 3, Y 5, Y Glide, Pro Issue DH.
- **SHOCK UNIT MAINTENANCE:** Regular air pressure check (on air/oil models), referring to a bike mechanic in case of constant air pressure loss.
- **INSTALLATION SIZE:** 160 mm (standard). The shock unit length is set for 80 mm of travel in front. If you use a front fork with more travel, it is recommended you also increase travel in the rear. Maximum shock unit installation size is 180 mm
- **TRAVEL:** 100 mm (standard), can be increased up to 135 mm. Special Trek parts are available for adjusting rear travel and bike geometry to the amount of travel to different front fork travel ratings.
- **ALTERNATE SHOCK UNITS:** Crane Creek AD 8, Noleen NR 3, Stratos Strata Shock Pro, and Rock Shox Coupe Deluxe. The bearing maintenance data apply to all Trek Y models, as well as to the Gary Fisher Joshua series.

BEARING REPLACEMENT

If the bearings feel loose or if there is damage to their bushings, particularly their Teflon coating, they must be replaced. Place the new bushing over the old one on the side and knock the new bushing in, which will push the old one out. This automatically places the main frame bushing into the right position. Stick the new side bushings in place with Loctite thread locking compound.

The pivot bushing set will set you back about U.S. $25.

MAINTENANCE TIPS

From time to time also clean the attachment lugs and the bushings of the shock unit. Use lubricant on these bushings. A very effective means of preventing or curing creaking noises in the shock unit attachment lugs is copper paste. For maintenance of the shock unit and rear triangle, you can use an ordinary bicycle cleaning oil such as the one made by Finish Line or even a mild soap solution. You can keep them clean by installing a neoprene or butyl protecting sleeve over the shock unit.

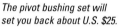

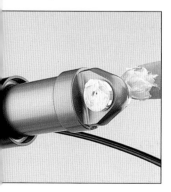

CABLE ROUTING AND SEATPOST

If you replace or reroute the cables to the rear triangle, take care not to make the outer cables too long. They get pushed in when the bike goes down on its suspension and if they're too long, they may get caught on the seat quick-release or other protruding shock unit parts.

Also beware if you like to lower your seat for downhill riding: Maintain at least 38 mm (1½ in.) between the bottom of the seatpost and the shock unit. Otherwise, the seatpost could do serious damage to the shock unit when the suspension is activated. You may consider simply shortening the seatpost so that none of it projects below the attachment clamp when the seat is in the highest position.

CANNONDALE SINGLE-PIVOT SUSPENSION

Sealed bearing single-pivot rear triangle designs, such as the one used by Cannondale, operate smoothly and require very little maintenance. Here's the little bit of maintenance they need.

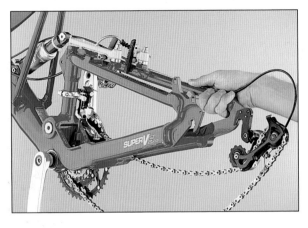

REAR TRIANGLE CHECK

Periodically check the rear triangle to determine the freedom of movement, which will reveal any problems with the bearing that may exist. To carry out this check, remove the rear bolt from the shock unit to free it from the rear triangle. The sealed bearing of the main pivot should be so smoothly running that you can twist the unit with the force of a single finger. Any lateral play can be due to one of two reasons: Either a loose spindle or a defective bearing. If it's a loose spindle, all you have to do is undo the central bolt, apply Loctite thread locking compound to the screw thread, and firmly tighten the bolt again.

BEARING CHECK

To check the condition of the bearing, first remove the right-hand crank, the chain, and all control cables to the rear triangle. Use two 8 mm Allen wrenches to unscrew the pivot bolt and remove both parts. Move the rear triangle up and down to remove it. Watch out for the shims between bearing bushings and the frame (the rear shim is clearly visible in the lower illustration, identified by the red arrow).

TECHNICAL DATA AND MAINTENANCE INTERVALS

- **REAR SUSPENSION TYPE:** Active single pivot swingarm.
- **BEARING TYPE:** Two double-sealed roller bearing units
- **BEARING DESIGNATION:** Industry standard 6903 RS (e.g. bearings made by SKS or FAG).
- **BEARING REPLACEMENT COST:** Around U.S. $15 for the pair.
- **BEARING MAINTENANCE INTERVAL:** Once every 6 months or 2,000 km (1,250 miles), but immediately if any problems occur (e.g. play, noise, etc.).
- **SHOCK UNIT:** Fox series (either air/oil or coil spring/oil).
- **SHOCK UNIT MAINTENANCE:** Regular air pressure check (on air/oil models), referring to a bike mechanic in case of constant air pressure loss. Annual oil change (coil spring/oil models).
- **INSTALLATION SIZE:** 165 mm for the Super VL series; 146 mm for the Raven and Super V Active series. The shock unit length is set for 80 mm of travel in front.
- **TRAVEL:** 120 mm (Super V SL series, Active 100 SL with Vanilla RX shock unit; 100 mm (Raven, Active 100 SL); 80 mm (Active 80). It is not possible to achieve longer travel through the installation of a longer shock unit.
- **ALTERNATE SHOCK UNITS:** All available models with the corresponding installation dimension (160 or 146 mm respectively). The bearing maintenance data apply to all Cannondale Super V models of model year 1996 or later, including Raven, and all downhill models.

BEARING MAINTENANCE

Even sealed bearing units sometimes should be repacked with lubricant. That increases their life expectancy significantly and should be made part of your maintenance routine. Even brand new sealed bearings often don't contain enough grease to withstand the ravages of the elements. Carefully lift off the neoprene seal on one side with a small screwdriver, working all around. Pack the space underneath in which the ball bearings lie tightly with bearing grease, then reseat the seal with your hand. This also protects the bearings against penetration of dirt and moisture.

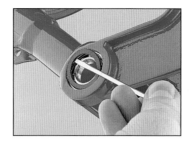

Medium-strength thread-lock compound, such as Loctite Blue, should be used wherever screwed connections should be held firmly in place in cases where vibrations might otherwise loosen them. This shows where to apply it on a pivot bearing unit.

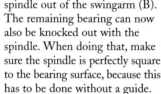

TUNING TIPS

The models with Fox Vanilla oil/air shock units require a high-pressure shock absorber air pump. First attach a ziptie to the damper piston rod. By means of releasing all air while compressing the shock unit, you can determine the total possible amount of shock unit travel. Once seated on the bike, the unit should compress by about one quarter to one third of this measure. That's what's called negative spring travel. Experiment with different pressures until you've established the optimum pressure for your rider weight.

Bikes equipped with coil spring/oil shock units: In this case, the spring rating is what matters most in terms of riding characteristics. The standard ex-factory configuration may or may not suit your rider weight, and you may have to replace the entire spring.

Fine tuning is achieved by adjusting the spring preload setting. Again, the correct adjustment is when the bike absorbs one third of its travel when the rider is seated passively on the bike.

BEARING REPLACEMENT

If the bearings feel loose or if there is noticeable play, they must be replaced. First bolt the spindle firmly down on one side of the bearing unit, making this side a guide for accurately removing the bearing on the other side with the aid of the spindle (see Fig. A). A few regular knocks with the plastic mallet will drive the spindle out of the swingarm (B). The remaining bearing can now also be knocked out with the spindle. When doing that, make sure the spindle is perfectly square to the bearing surface, because this has to be done without a guide.

The new bearings can usually be pushed into place at least partly by hand. Then use a fitting piece of tubing to knock them in all the way until the top is flush with the outside of the swingarm unit. To do this, make sure that the piece of tubing or whatever aid you use lies on the outer race of the bearing, otherwise you wll damage the bearing. Later, when you install the rear triangle in the frame, the bearings will be pushed all the way into their seating by tightening the spindle. The recommended tightening torque is given by Cannondale as 45 Nm (Newton-meter), or 20 ftlb (foot-pound).

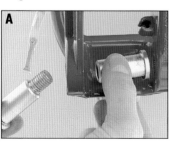

A

B

C

SPECIALIZED FOUR-BAR LINKAGE

Four-bar linkages with journal bearings require more care and maintenance than other rear suspension designs. You can only get the full benefit of this design if you check these units frequently and fix anything before it gets out of hand. Here you'll find typical procedures for all such devices shown by the example of the Specialized design.

PIVOT BEARING MAINTENANCE

On account of its exposed location behind the bottom bracket, the main pivot bearing sees a lot of dirt and water, so it also requires frequent and thorough maintenance. To work on this bearing, first remove the right-hand crank. In order to overhaul any of the other pivot bearings, we recommend also removing the chain and any cables that run to the rear portion of the bike.

Loosen the bushing on the right-hand side of the main bearing, using an 8 mm Allen wrench, while countering the one on the left side with a 6 mm Allen wrench. Next knock the left-hand bushing out by hitting it carefully with a mallet and a punch, working all around.

Clean all contact surfaces thoroughly but don't apply grease to this self-lubricating bearing, although it's OK to apply a drop of thick oil and spread it over the bearing surfaces. When reassembling, use Loctite thread-lock compound on the screw thread to prevent unintentional loosening of the bolts. All other bearings are handled the same way—they're just smaller.

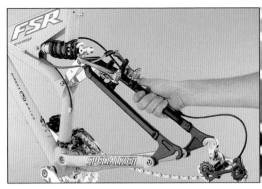

REAR TRIANGLE CHECK

Remove the rear wheel and loosen the lower pivot point of the shock unit. You should now be able to move the entire rear structure up and down, hinged at its pivot points. When new, the journal bearings of the Specialized FSR models offer rather high resistance, but it should remain constant over the entire range of movement, and the resistance decreases with use. However, there should always be some detectable resistance—if not, it will be time to replace the bearing bushings, as is also the case when you notice creaking sounds or uneven operation. Also check for lateral play: You should not be able to move the rear unit sideways.

TECHNICAL DATA AND MAINTENANCE INTERVALS

- **REAR SUSPENSION TYPE:** Active four-bar linkage.
- **BEARING TYPE:** Carbon-fiber-reinforced polymer journal bearings.
- **BEARING REPLACEMENT COST:** Bushing set around U.S. $25; spindle set around U.S. $40.
- **BEARING MAINTENANCE INTERVAL:** Once every 6 months or 2,000 km (1,250 miles), but immediately if any problems occur (e.g. play, noise, etc.).
- **SHOCK UNIT:** Rock Shox Deluxe (coil spring/oil) for FSR Comp model; Fox Vanilla (coil spring/oil) for FSR model; Fox Vanilla R (coil spring/oil) for FSR Elite model.
- **SHOCK UNIT MAINTENANCE:** Regular air pressure check (on air/oil models), referring to a bike mechanic in case of constant air pressure loss. Annual oil change (coil spring/oil models).
- **INSTALLATION SIZE:** 150 mm (standard). Shock travel is set for use with a front fork with 80 mm of travel.
- **TRAVEL:** 110 mm (standard). It is not possible to achieve longer travel through the installation of a longer shock unit.
- **ALTERNATE SHOCK UNITS:** Specialized uses non-standard Rock Shox and Fox shock units that are specifically designed for the FSR. Consequently, it is recommended to use only shock units obtained through a Specialized dealer for use with the FSR.

BEARING REPLACEMENT

Replacing the bearings of this kind of rear unit is really a job for a specialist, and we don't recommend you try this yourself unless you are a very experienced mechanic and have the appropriate manual and tools. The job takes about two hours.

In case of play in the bearings, the first thing to do is replace the white plastic bushings. The pivot pins themselves are not due for replacement until you've worn out three sets of plastic bushings or when the anodized layer of the pin is noticeably worn, revealing the much brighter bare aluminum.

First separate the bearing by loosening the Allen bolts. Then push or knock the pins out using a blunt object, like a punch and a mallet. The plastic bushings are held tightly in the aluminum and should be knocked out very carefully. It's very important to start installing the new bushings exactly square to the surface and to protect them with a block of wood instead of hitting them directly with the mallet. Another way to do it is to press them in using a C-clamp (the kind of thing woodworkers use to keep glued parts together). Remember not to use grease when working on a Specialized full-suspension bike or any other model with plastic bushings. Secure the screw threads of the bolts with Loctite thread-lock compound and tighten them by hand only.

THE SEATPOST

On Specialized full-suspension bikes, there's a little hole near the bottom of the seat tube through which the seatpost should be visible. If not, you should replace it by a longer model to suit your size. In order to remove any excess length to prevent damaging the rear shock unit when the seatpost is lowered for downhill riding, first place the seat in the highest position for your normal riding, then mark the seatpost through the hole. Remove the seatpost and cut off at about 3 mm (1¼ in.) below the marking, using a tubing cutter.

CARE INSTRUCTIONS

The attachment bushings, the rod, and the housing lugs of the shock unit should all be cleaned and lightly greased from time to time. The best way to wash the unit is with a mild soap and water.

And here's a do-it-yourself protective sleeve for the linkages: Push sections of bicycle inner tube over the linkages and tie them down at both ends with zipties.

TUNING TIPS

FACTORY SETTING:
Frame sizes S and M: Spring rating 650 lbs/in.: rider weight 59–72 kg (130–160 kg).
RH L: Spring rating 75 lbs/in.: rider weight 68–81 kg (150–180 lbs) Models FSR Com/Extreme.
The factory settings for the Elite and Pro models are about 50 lbs higher than the values listed above.

TUNING:
Riders weighing between 50 and 63 kg (110 and 140 lbs respectively) should use a 600 lb/in. spring, possibly even one rated at 550 lb/in. Very heavy riders, on the other hand, should choose a spring rated at least 850 lb/in.

SHOCK THERAPY

Out in terrain, the rear wheel often works as a "muckraker," and much of that muck heads straight for the rear suspension shock unit. Regular and preventive maintenance keeps the shock unit working smoothly.

I. PIVOT BUSHING MAINTENANCE

It's an established fact that rear shocks often deteriorate quickly as a result of dirt and moisture penetration when in use out in the open terrain. You can easily prevent these problems with regular care.

Although ball-bearing bushings are no longer a rarity, most bikes still make do with journal bearings. Here, dirt particles—often mixed with moisture—can penetrate into the bushings and cause excessive resistance in the pivots. Often the Teflon "maintenance-free" surfaces get damaged and the shock stops rotating with the suspension, eventually causing damage to the unit itself.

Remove the shock unit once or twice a season and clean all bearing contact surfaces, as well as the unit itself. Unscrew the 6 or 8 mm Allen bolts, countering at the other side with an open-ended wrench (see Fig. 1a), and then lift the unit out (see Fig. 1b). Note that the nut on the other side is usually a locking insert nut (see Fig. 1c). Those are strictly "one-way" nuts: Throw out the old ones and replace them with new ones of the same type and size. Don't forget to do that, even when you're only removing the coil spring.

The bushings can usually be removed and installed by hand (see Fig. 1c). If they are too tight to be pulled out by hand, you can use a small screwdriver as a lever to pry them out. After you have cleaned the inner surfaces of the shock's attachment lugs (see Fig. 1d), lightly lubricate the bushings with a lithium-free lubricant, such as Gold-Slick, and replace the bushings by hand (see Figs. 1e and 1f). Don't be tempted to replace the bolts by lightweight ones: Only steel is strong enough for this kind of service.

1a

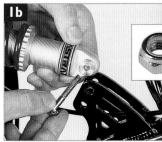
1b

1c

1d

1e

1f

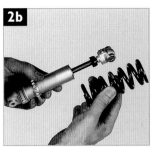

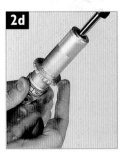

2. PISTON ROD INSPECTION

The damper piston rod of coil-spring shock units is hard to reach. In order to inspect it, you'll have to remove the entire unit from the bike. That's done as described above for removal of the spring unit. Many shocks require the adjusting screw to be removed in order to slide the spring off over the top of the unit (see Fig. 2a). While you're there, apply some penetrating oil to the adjuster screw thread so it will be easily adjustable.

Next, release the preload until the coil spring is loose enough to move the slotted spring support dish toward the top (see Fig 2b). The black ring which is now exposed is not the main seal but a boot that serves to prevent the penetration of dirt and water, and it can easily be removed (see Fig. 2c). Often there will be a thin film of oil on the piston rod. We suggest you also apply a little lubricant to the preload screw and screw thread, which prevents nasty sounds and provides ease of adjustment (see Fig. 2d).

3. VALVE REPLACEMENT

Most air-sprung shock units are equipped with a Schrader valve. Usually, there's a metal dust cap installed on top, and we recommend you keep it there. If the unit loses air pressure constantly, it's often due to a leaky valve. It's easy to remove and replace the valve using a special Schrader valve tool (fig. 3a), available at any automotive parts store. Simply grab the valve unit inside with the slotted tool and unscrew it (see Fig. 3b). The replacement valve gets installed the same way.

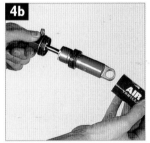

FOX AIR VANILLA NOTE

As opposed to other air-sprung shocks, these have a small-diameter piston rod similar to what's found on a coil spring unit. What looks like the housing is no more than an enclosure to keep out dirt and to keep the internals protected, sliding up-and-down over the actual housing over a large-diameter seal. This seal often gets dried out, causing friction and reducing the unit's response rate.

To lubricate the seal, carefully clamp the installation lug (on the large-diameter side) and unscrew the cover off the fine screw thread (see Fig. 4a). Then pull it off so you have access to the seal to apply lubricant. Reinstall in reverse sequence.

THE NEOPRENE SLEEVE SOLUTION

Although placing a neoprene protective sleeve over the shock unit seems like a good idea, there's a drawback as well: There's a risk of "out of sight, out of mind." You don't want water, dust, and grit building up under that protector sleeve. The only place to use it is over a coil spring unit (see Fig. 5a). Don't use these devices on air-sprung shocks, because dirt can build up inside it and scratch the smooth surfaces (see Fig. 5b). Instead, wash your shock unit frequently with soapy water and a soft brush. And if you think you have to use a hose, steer away from the seals with the water jet.

10 OPTIMIZING SUSPENSION AND DAMPING

Even the best full-suspension bike loses all its agility when it's not properly matched to the rider. This chapter shows easy ways to help you get the most of your full-suspension bike.

Compression phase, spring rate, preload, stiction—a seemingly endless stream of new terms are being hurled at the innocent mountain biker trying to come to terms with his or her suspension system. Especially the more expensive models amongst full-suspension bikes offer a multitude of knobs, buttons, and valves to control individual characteristics of the suspension system components. If you start changing those various settings without knowing what each one really achieves, you may soon find yourself riding what seems more like a bolting horse than a finely tuned full-suspension bike. Improperly adjusted, even the best full-suspension mountain bike will actually be harder to ride than a simple machine without suspension.

The most common mistake amongst novice full-suspension riders is to set the spring rate too high, resulting in a ride that's far from comfortable on steep downhill sections. The only thing that then reminds you of the fact that you got a full-suspension bike is the higher weight.

There are a number of different ways to achieve a perfectly tuned suspension system. The first, and least expensive, option is to buy a bike with minimal tuning and adjusting options. Full-suspension bikes in the price range between U.S. $1,000 and $2,000 are usually set up by the manufacturer in a pretty sensible and universally agreeable configuration—but without the opportunity for the rider to make many personalized adjustments.

The second option is to find a bike shop with employees who understand the subject matter so well that they can set up the bike accurately to your personal needs, both when you first buy it and later as you become more experienced riding it. That works fine if that bike shop is close by where you live, but not so useful if you live in the middle of nowhere—great for riding but far from a good bike shop.

The third, and in the long run the most satisfying, option is to familiarize yourself with the subject matter and learn enough about the physics of the moving bike and its suspension and damping systems to set it up correctly yourself.

When you get right down to it, it's all a matter of finding the correct balance between suspension and damping. Unfortunately, those two concepts are only too often confused, so let's try to understand them properly.

Let's look at suspension first. From a physics standpoint, suspension is a method of storing energy. When the wheel encounters an obstacle, the suspension is pushed in, and the spring element (whether air spring, elastomer pads, or coil spring) is pushed in, storing the energy in the form of what's referred to as potential energy. If undamped, the spring then would want to release this stored potential energy as soon as possible in the form of kinetic (i.e. movement) energy, making the bike bounce up. Basically, the suspension isolates the sprung mass (the weight of the rider and the main part of the frame) from the unsprung mass (the wheels and the lower parts of the suspension elements). The unsprung mass should follow the contours of the ground as closely as possible, while the sprung mass should "float" above it with a minimum of jolts.

Two distinct advantages are associated with this separation of sprung and unsprung masses: rider comfort and better traction. The well-suspended rider doesn't get knocked about so much, allowing him or her to concentrate on steering the bike. Since the wheels closely follow the contours of the ground, the rider's input is immediately translated into reactions from the bike; after all, steering, braking, and accelerating only work when the wheels are actually in contact with the ground, and that's what suspension achieves.

Of particular importance for traction is what's referred to as "sag" (in essence, it could be seen as the negative spring rate—the amount of travel that is taken up with the rider just sitting on the bike). Sag represents the ability of the suspension to push the wheel back onto the ground when riding through a deep spot or after it's been raised up over a bump. On average, sag should be around 30 percent of total travel. For

COMPARING SUSPENSION SET-UPS

Upper diagram: Insufficient rebound damping. Although the unsprung masses (the wheels) can follow the surface irregularities quickly enough, the bike bounces up and down too much due to inadequate damping on the rebound, causing the wheels to start losing contact with the surface, resulting in diminished traction. Lower diagram: Properly adjusted damping. The tires closely follow the surface bumps and maintain their ground contact, maintaining traction. The bike does not see-saw, and the rider is largely isolated from surface impacts.

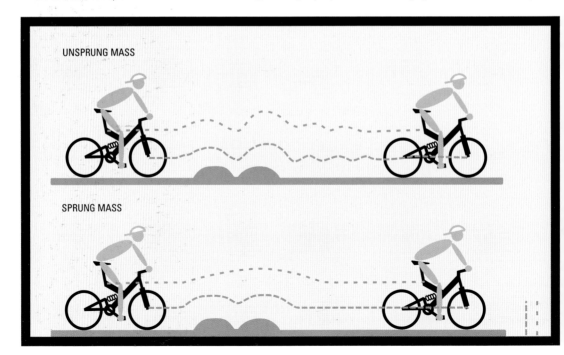

UNSPRUNG MASS

SPRUNG MASS

cross-country competition, the amount of sag should be around 15 to 20 percent, while for downhill racing rear suspension sag should be as much as 40 percent, due to the forward displacement of rider's weight on steep downhill sections.

For air/oil shocks, the air pressure is critically important for correct tuning. Adhere to the manufacturer's recommendations for the appropriate rider weight.

On coil spring suspension units, front or rear, sag is adjusted by selecting a stronger or softer spring and by means of adjusting the amount of preload. Keep in mind that preload adjustment should only be used for fine-tuning within the target zone and should not replace the selection of the right spring associated with the particular rider weight and the amount of desired sag. You're working with the wrong spring if you have to tighten the preload adjuster on the shock unit by more than five turns to get the amount of desired sag. Select a spring with a higher rating instead (coil springs are rated in lbs/in. and are available in 50 lb/in. increments in the range between 500 and 850 lb/in. for most models). On air-sprung units, sag adjustment is easier because there's no preload and the spring rate can be adjusted gradually by increasing or decreasing the air pressure.

When you buy a new full-suspension bike, the people at the bike shop should set you up with the right spring for your body weight and the kind of riding you plan to do. If they don't take the trouble to check it out in an effort to make a quick sale, let them know you want it done because you know how important it is but haven't figured out how to do it yourself. If the bike shop is any good, they should be happy to do it for you and explain how you can check and/or modify the setting for yourself if conditions change.

On most suspension forks, the preload adjuster knobs are located above the fork crown on top of the stanchions. To adjust for the correct amount of sag, first determine the maximum amount of travel.

But first a few words about damping. As mentioned before, a spring functions as an energy-storage device, and once it's moving, it has a tendency to keep bouncing up and down. That's what happens with a pogo stick, but it's not what you want your bike to do. This is where damping comes in: Damping reduces the rebound reaction and consequently the "bounciness" of the suspension. On oil-damped units, that's achieved by connecting the two ends of the spring via a piston with one or more small openings that's forced through an oil-filled cylinder. It turns some of that stored energy from the spring into heat. The trick is to set the damper up in such a way that the faster the movement of the spring, the bigger the damping effect should be. On most elastomer-sprung forks, the damping is also achieved by means of some configuration of elastomer pads—

a cheaper solution that's not as responsive and easy to adjust (a matter of replacing pads and bumpers inside the unit), but requires little maintenance and generally suitable for riders who don't want to bother too much with the mechanics of their bikes.

There are two distinct damping stages: Compression stage damping slows the reaction when the suspension is pushed in, and rebound damping slows the bouncing back when released. Compression stage damping mainly serves to prevent bottoming out the suspension unit when it is compressed, so it

GLOSSARY

- **SUSPENSION:** Suspension works as an energy-storage device. When force is applied to the spring, it stores potential engergy, which is later released in the form of kinetic (i.e. movement) energy. The most commonly used spring elements are coil springs, elastomers, and compressed air.

- **DAMPING:** Damping works as a brake on the movements of a suspension unit. Oil is the most common medium for damping elements on suspension forks and rear shocks. When the spring is compressed or released, a piston with holes (valves) is pushed through the oil cylinder, converting kinetic energy to heat energy and slowing the spring movements.

- **COMPRESSION STAGE DAMPING:** The compression stage damping controls the speed of pushing in the spring of a suspension unit upon impact.

- **REBOUND DAMPING:** Rebound damping controls the speed of the spring in a suspension element when it recovers from initial impact.

- **SAG:** Also called negative spring travel, Sag is the amount of a suspension element's travel taken up before any impact is applied to it, i.e. with just the rider weight on the bike.

- **RESPONSE RATE:** The higher the response rate, the more sensitive a suspension element is to forces applied to it.

- **STICTION:** The initial force needed to effect any movement at all in a suspension element.

doesn't really contribute much to increasing traction control. Rebound damping, on the other hand, is very important for traction and safety, helping the wheel stay in contact with the ground after the initial impact. If the tire frequently loses contact with the ground, it's usually due to inadequate rebound damping, and the bike will tend to see-saw as it reacts to a bump. If the suspension gets less and less effective during a bumpy ride due to its inability to recover fully from each consecutive impact, it will be due to excessive rebound damping.

Unfortunately, there's not one optimal setting for damping that's best for any type of terrain. The basic setting to which the bike is adjusted in the bike shop is a good starting point, but beyond

The better your bike's suspension and damping are tuned to match the type of terrain you ride in, the faster and safer will be your ride.

that, it's a matter of trial and error. Find a good stretch of varied terrain that will be representative of most of the kind of riding you plan to do. It should contain plenty of the real-life situations

you expect to encounter on the trail: rippled surfaces, bigger bumps, gullies, jumps, steep downhill sections, climbing in even and bumpy terrain, compacted, rocky, and loose surfaces, plenty of curves, etc.

Once you've found the right test course, all you need is plenty of energy and determination— and a systematic approach with painstaking record-keeping discipline. First traverse the test stretch a couple of times with the bike set up the way it is. This will establish a point of departure to which you can compare any modifications you carry out. Once you have a feel for it, make one adjustment, and only one at a time. The best place to start is by first increasing compression stage damping. If it improves the situation, try increasing it a little more, until things start to get worse, and then back off a little until you've found the optimum amount of compression stage damping.

Ideally, your bike should be set up to handle the most typical sit-

uations, and that means there will be "extreme" situations when e.g. the suspension "bottoms out." It's best when that happens just once during your traversing of the test circuit. If it doesn't bottom out once, you've not set it up optimally for the most typical situations; and if it bottoms out several times, you're operating too close to the limit of the suspension's ability to absorb shocks.

Once you've found the optimum setting for compression stage damping, proceed to the next variable, e.g. rebound damping, working in stages the same way as before. An excellent way of establishing a good adjustment to start off with is to simply sit on the bike and let it roll down a curb, keeping track of the number of times the bike bops up and down afterwards. If just once, you're pretty close to the optimum rebound damping; if it see-saws several times, rebound damping is inadequate and should be increased. Work on this, closing the rebound damping adjuster until it bops up just once. For fine-tuning, go back to the test circuit and work on it until you've found the right setting. There's too much rebound damping if the bike loses traction when traversing "washboard" rippled surfaces, with the suspension getting more and more compressed, and the amount of travel diminishing over time. If, on the other hand, the bike starts to swing out of control on longish surface bumps and dips, like waves, it will be an indication that you've got too little rebound damping.

When doing these various tests, keep in mind that it's best to retain a kind of balance between the front and rear suspension; so each time, you should make the same adjustments to the front and rear units. Quite often any undesirable suspension system reactions are due to an uneven distribution between front and rear settings. So keep things even until you've found

TIPS & TRICKS

- The most important rule about full-suspension bike tuning: Proceed step by step. Never change more than one variable at a time between test rides. If you change more, you won't know which of them had the effect you notice.
- The secret about suspension tuning is to establish a delicate balance between suspension and damping functions of the front and rear suspension units, which should be evenly distributed.
- Increased preload does not necessarily imply higher spring tension. A highly preloaded spring doesn't change the spring characteristics themselves: It just diminishes response rate. If you have to preload a spring too much, you should replace it by a stronger one instead.

Often a minor problem can have a big impact on a bike's riding characteristics. With a few simple corrective measures, you can optimize your full-suspension bike's handling. Listed here are the most common problems and what you can do to correct them.

The suspension dives frequently and often bottoms out. The spring rate is too low.

If it's an air/oil unit, increase the air pressure. If it's a coil spring unit, increase the spring's preload. But beware: Increasing the preload is of only limited benefit when it comes to adjusting the shock to the rider's weight. Excessive preload adjustment reduces response rate and increases stiction. The only complete solution is the installation of a stronger spring.

The suspension is not responsive; the total available amount of travel is not used up.

The spring rate is too high for the rider's weight. If it's an air/oil unit, let some air out to reduce the pressure. On other models, reduce preload. If the spring rate is still too high after this correction, it should be replaced by a lower rated spring. Another possible cause is excessive compression stage damping. Check both possibilities.

The suspension keeps getting compressed more and more in response to short, fast bumps, and recovers only slowly.

This phenomenon is common on washboard surfaces and trails with lots of tree roots going across. It's caused by excessive rebound damping. Undo the preload damping adjuster gradually until the bike absorbs short, fast bumps without becoming hard to control.

The bike becomes "restless" at higher speeds. The tires lose ground contact on longer surface undulations.

This is caused by too little rebound damping, causing the full range of travel to be reached too early. Tighten the rebound damping adjuster a little at a time and keep testing the bike on the same stretch of trail until the wheels keep constant contact with the ground.

The suspension gets harder in response to short, fast bumps.

This is caused by a compression stage that is too hard. If the suspension unit is equipped with compression stage adjustment, open it up in small steps until the desired characteristics are reached. Otherwise, have it checked by a suspension specialist workshop or use a different model.

Although the rear suspension works just fine, the front end of the bike feels hard and insensitive.

This kind of unbalanced riding characteristics suggest that the suspension fork and the rear suspension are poorly matched to each other. An example would be combining an elastomer front fork with a mere 60 mm (2⅜ in.) of travel with a high-performance rear shock unit with coil spring and 12 cm (4¾ in.) of travel. This problem can be solved by upgrading the fork with a long-travel kit or a coil-spring upgrade kit.

The rear end of the bike suddenly gets out of control and begins to bounce.

The most likely cause is a defective damping unit on the rear shock. Check the rear unit for traces of oil, especially around the piston rod. If you don't find traces of oil, remove the shock unit and remove the coil spring. Then check the resistance of the damper by pushing the piston rod in and out. If there's very little resistance, it should be overhauled or replaced.

The bike tracks poorly in curves as though the tires are not inflated properly.

This is usually due to excessive play in the pivot bearings of the rear triangle. Check the pivot bearings and have the bushings and/or pivot spindles replaced if necessary.

The rear suspension or the front fork has lost much of its original responsiveness.

Most likely the bearings, seals, and bushings in the fork and/or the rear triangle are gummed up with greasy dirt. Remove the shock unit and/or the spring element from the front fork. Now move the rear triangle or the front suspension unit up and down. If this movement requires significant hand force, it's time to clean the bearings, pivots, and/or seals. But follow the manufacturer's instructions to the letter.

what seems like a good overall response, and only then try slightly increasing or decreasing the settings of the front relative to the rear to establish whether this will give your settings the final touch— or until you are convinced that you have arrived at the best balance of suspension and damping.

Once you've set up the bike properly, give yourself enough time to get used ot it set up that way. After a month or so, you will have become so aware of the bike's behavior that you can detect small changes. At this point, decide whether there are certain characteristics you want to fine-tune. If that's the case, go back to the same test circuit and repeat the tests, this time only adjusting what you think you want to improve. Work just as systematically until you're certain you've got the best settings for your current riding style.

SHOCK UNIT REPLACEMENT

If your rear shock unit is obviously defective or no longer works to your satisfaction, it's time to replace it with a new unit. Another reason to replace it is when you can't set up the existing unit correctly to match the rider's weight. Here are the four criteria that are important to consider when buying a replacement shock unit:

1. INSTALLATION LENGTH: Your bike's design determines the installation length that will fit. If the new shock unit is shorter than the original, the bike will move closer to the ground and that will result in insufficient travel. Only bikes with variable installation lugs allow a little latitude in the length of the shock unit you can install.

2. INSTALLATION WIDTH: This dimension should be measured with calipers and care should be exercised to use only exactly fitting replacement units and matching bushings. Don't try to make up missing millimeters by inserting spacing washers.

3. TRAVEL: Even if the installation length is the same, there can still be a difference in the amount of travel. The amount of travel determines the distance over which the rear triangle can move up and down (it also depends on the relative locations of rear wheel and shock unit attachments). If the new unit results in increased travel of the rear triangle, you must check to make sure the rear triangle doesn't touch the main frame or the seat post anywhere.

4. BOLT DIAMETER: The installation bolts also come in various diameters (usually either 6 mm or 8 mm). Also make sure the bolts don't have any screw thread in the center portion, so they don't cut into the aluminum bushings.

HOW TO ADJUST SAG (NEGATIVE SPRING TRAVEL)

The amount of sag must be selected to match the rider's weight and the kind of use for the bike. This is one of the basic adjustments for any full-suspension bike. This is how it's done:

I-2. First measure the height of the saddle above the rear wheel axle without any weight applied to the bike. Then sit on the bike, supporting yourself with one hand against a wall; distribute your weight over the seat and

the handlebars as you would when riding. Then have a helper measure the difference in height between seat and rear axle with the bike loaded this way.

3. Remove the shock unit and remove the coil spring. To do that, you'll have to undo the installation

bolt, loosen the preload screw, and remove the dish-shaped spring support. Then reinstall the shock unit without the spring (see page 80).

4. Now it's possible to measure the maximum spring travel. After this measurement is completed, you can reinstall the spring in the shock unit and then the shock unit back in the bike. Although this method is rather time-consuming, it is by far the most reliable

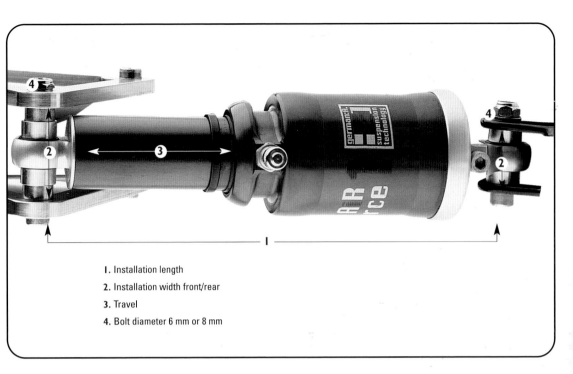

1. Installation length
2. Installation width front/rear
3. Travel
4. Bolt diameter 6 mm or 8 mm

method of determining the actual amount of rear travel on bikes with coil spring/oil shock units.

The amount of preload should now be set at a value ranging from 15 to 20 percent of travel for cross-country up to 40 percent for downhill and freeride use.

5. It's much easier to determine the amount of travel on a front suspension fork and air/oil rear shocks. This is where you get to use the previously explained ziptie method. Establish the total amount of travel by removing the end caps on top of the stanchion tubes and simply let the air out at the valves. Then you can mark the amount of travel as the distance between the ziptie positions in inflated and deflated conditions.

6. Use the preload adjuster knobs to set the required amount of sag, or negative spring travel, to correspond to your body weight and the kind of use you have in mind (see point 4 above).

OVERVIEW OF
BRAKE SYSTEMS

To ride fast, you have to be able to stop fast as well. These days, there are plenty of choices in braking systems and components for mountain bike use. In addition to the common V-brake, there are both hydraulic caliper brakes and disk brakes.

The question of what kind of brake you want to use should come up as soon as you contemplate buying a new bike or a bare frame. Unlike the early days of mountain biking, there are now several distinct types of very satisfactory brake systems available. All of them are controlled by means of hand-operated levers on the handlebars, but that's where similarities end.

Most common amongst mountain bike brakes, and the most economical source for average use, is the V-brake, which works on the sides of the rim. They can be thought of as elongated versions of the once popular cantilever brakes, giving more leverage due to their greater length. Each brake arm has a pivot point at the bottom, terminates in a cable attachment at the top, and has a brake pad mounted somewhere in between. The cable housing terminates at the top of one, and the inner cable runs through to the other brake arm. Pulling the lever pulls the top of the brake arms, pushing the brake pads against the rim to slow down the bike.

In the hydraulic operation of brakes, the conventional cable link between levers and brake units are replaced by hydraulic tubes. Because there is (virtually) no resistance in hydraulic lines, they provide smoother operation and a more direct response than cable brakes. The only even remotely common hydraulically operated caliper brake (i.e. a brake that works on the sides of the rim, like most cable-operated mountain bike brakes) is the one made by Magura.

The trend amongst downhill and freeride bikes, however, is disk brakes. Similar to those used on cars and motorcycles, they comprise a thin steel disk connected to the wheel hub, on which a pair of callipers act to slow down the bike. Most of these are hydraulically operated, although some models use cables for part of the connection between lever and caliper.

In recent years, many manufacturers of frames and forks have started to equip certain models with attachment lugs and screw-threaded bosses welded onto the frame for use with disk brakes. That's a good thing too, because these brakes apply so much reaction force to the frame or the fork that attaching them with makeshift devices is asking for trouble. In fact, the tubes themselves have to be strong and stiff enough to stand up to the reaction forces when braking. Don't "upgrade" a bike that wasn't designed to accept disk brakes.

Most disk brakes now have mounting hardware that is dimensioned to conform to the international standard, although there is a slight difference between the early (1999) and the more recent (2000) standards (for an explanation, see page 98).

All other brakes can be installed on the conventional bosses provided for cantilever brakes. There are some older brake types, no longer in use but still found on some older bikes, that use non-standard boss positions. Thus, if you want to replace one of those old U-brakes or Power-Cam brakes, you'll find that modern brakes don't fit. Sorry, but it was about time you replaced that old frame or fork anyway...

Although an old idea, V-brakes really took over with the proliferation of suspension bikes: They allow for easier cable routing and don't require outer cable stops that are so difficult to combine with suspension forks and frames—a detail that not only removes some of the cluttered appearance, but also makes life easier on frame designers.

More problematic is matching the brake to the lever. Of course, the easiest option, and the one chosen by most manufacturers, is to combine brakes and levers from the same Shimano gruppo: For example, XTR brake levers and XTR V-brakes work perfectly together. Beyond that, there are lots of small manufacturers who make nicely CNC-machined brakes, and it can be hard to find a pair of levers that matches them (the amount of lever travel must match the leverage at the brake, and conven-

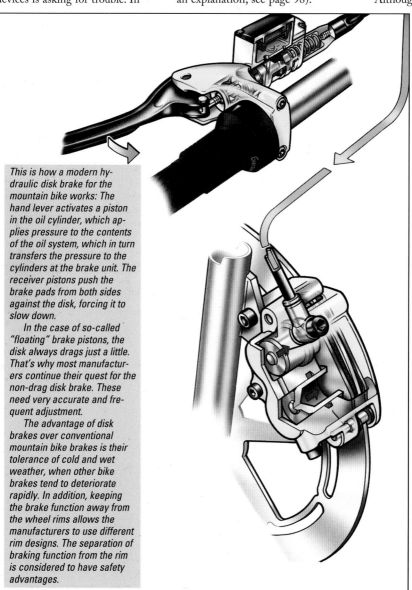

This is how a modern hydraulic disk brake for the mountain bike works: The hand lever activates a piston in the oil cylinder, which applies pressure to the contents of the oil system, which in turn transfers the pressure to the cylinders at the brake unit. The receiver pistons push the brake pads from both sides against the disk, forcing it to slow down.

In the case of so-called "floating" brake pistons, the disk always drags just a little. That's why most manufacturers continue their quest for the non-drag disk brake. These need very accurate and frequent adjustment.

The advantage of disk brakes over conventional mountain bike brakes is their tolerance of cold and wet weather, when other bike brakes tend to deteriorate rapidly. In addition, keeping the brake function away from the wheel rims allows the manufacturers to use different rim designs. The separation of braking function from the rim is considered to have safety advantages.

The classic amongst mountain bike anchors: Shimano's XTR V-brake. Unlike most cheaper models, these brakes are equipped with a linkage mechanism to keep the pads properly aligned with the sides of the rim. Great performance and easy adjustability.

can cause. Magura's hydraulic brakes are easily fitted to standard brake bosses and work like anchors, while still being sensitive enough to allow the rider some discretion over just how fast he or she wants the bike to decelerate. Although hydraulics require some maintenance (the liquid-filled lines have to be flushed out and "bled" from time to time to remove air bubbles which make operation "spongy"), they've proven at least as reliable as conventional cable-operated brakes. Even replacing the brake pads is quite easy on the Magura hydraulic brakes, and they're available in several different compounds to match different rim materials and weather conditions.

V-brakes and hydraulic caliper brakes have one disadvantage in common: They wear down on the sides of the wheel rims, and left unchecked, this can lead to cracks in the rim surface, and in extreme cases even to sudden wheel collapse. The best advise is not to choose the lightest rims if your bike uses rim brakes. Slightly heavier rims are also much more likely to stay round anyway (so you don't have to true the wheels as frequently). Anyway, we're really

tional cantilever brakes and V-brakes have entirely different leverage profiles). There have been some reports that the Shimano XTR brakes, with matching levers, provide so much stopping power, that a novice rider is apt to jettison him- or herself clean over the handlebars. If you're seriously worried about that risk, perhaps you want to use Shimano's lower-priced versions, which are

thought to be a little more forgiving. Other manufacturers offer similarly powerful V-brakes—as long as you use them in combination with the same manufacturer's matching levers.

Other brake types combine the brake efficiency of V-brakes without the drag that cable-operation

BRAKE SYSTEMS COMPARED

Brake type	V-brakes	Hydraulic caliper brakes	Disk brakes
Advantages	powerful braking low hand force application point easy to adjust relatively good modulation special brake pads available	powerful braking easy to adjust good modulation special brake pads available low maintenance reliable	very powerful braking low hand force good modulation, depending on specific model no rim wear low maintenance
Disadvantages	application sometimes too direct, depending on brake lever used requires specific brake lever high rim wear sometimes noisy	application point not easy to detect (difficult for beginners) complicated initial installation difficult to repair higher weight	very complicated to install higher weight expensive does not fit every model bike or fork difficult to repair

These problems are eliminated with the use of disk brakes, because the disks are the only things that wear out, other than the brake pads, without affecting the integrity of the wheels. As is the case with their big brothers used on motor cycles and cars, the most expensive disk brakes are hydraulically operated, while models for less rigorous use may be cable-operated, and some models use a combination of these two methods.

Closed system hydraulic-operated disk brakes are considered "state of the art" nowadays. They usually have an equalizing reservoir that almost eliminates the need for venting, bleeding, and topping off the hydraulic liquid. Even the once unavoidable energy-consuming and irritating habit of disk brakes to drag (even when you're not pulling the brake lever) is slowly becoming a thing of the past. Even so, most disk brakes are heavier and more complicated (not to mention their price penalty) than V-brakes, and it should be stated here that they only come into their own in downhill riding. Why would you want to spend all that extra money to get a brake that holds you back when every bit of effort is your own input, as it is in most riding situations other than downhill competition. (That, however, is a situation that may be changing, because

Technically well-conceived and with good modulation, Magura's hydraulic caliper brakes are an excellent choice. Their main disadvantage is that there's not much you can do yourself if they fail out on a ride, such as when the hydraulic fuel tubing bursts.

some manufacturers are producing lighter brakes that are claimed to be drag-free.)

For the most practical, reliable, and trouble-free everyday braking situation, it is hard to beat the effectiveness and simplicity of the V-brake. They're cheap, easy to adjust, their condition is easily checked, their cables and brake pads are easily replaced, and their spare parts can easily be carried around, even out on the trail.

If you're not satisfied with the performance of your rim brake, ask about alternate brake pad materials for the specific type of rim used on your bike. Sometimes brake performance can be improved up to 50 percent by selecting the right combination of rim and brake pad.

only talking about a few ounces one way or the other. Even regular rims, but especially lightweight rims, should frequently be inspected and replaced when they show cracks or excessive wear on the sides.

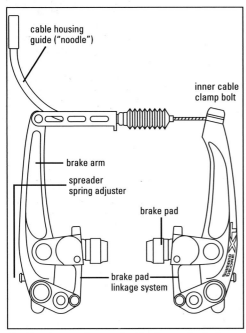

cable housing guide ("noodle")

inner cable clamp bolt

brake arm

spreader spring adjuster

brake pad

brake pad linkage system

The V-brake owes its great braking force to its design characteristics: The brake pads are pushed against the sides of the rim with the leverage provided by the long brake arms, to which the cables are attached directly. Due to the linkage system used, Shimano XTR and Deore XT brakes keep the brake pads aligned with the rim so they make contact over their entire area.

I. INADEQUATE BRAKE FORCE

First check the application point. If it seems too weak or if the lever can be pushed in nearly all the way to the handlebars, the inadequate performance is probably due to a problem with the hydraulic system. Bleed the hydraulic system and check. If it continues to get weaker, check the system for leaks. Replace as needed. Otherwise, the following measures will help:

- Most brake levers are installed too close to the ends of the handlebars. Move them far enough from the handlebar ends to assure you grip them at the ends so you can apply more force.
- There is a wide variety of aftermarket brake pads available, but they don't always make things better, and their installation may well void your warranty. It is better to stick with the ones offered by the original brake manufacturer. We've seen aftermarket pads that seemed to improve performance briefly—only to disintegrate after some time, leaving the rider in a lurch.
- If you do want to experiment with other pads, take particular care to match the brake pad material to the disk material. The major difference is between organic pad materials and sintered materials, and the disk materials differ correspondingly. If you use sintered pads on a disk designed for organic pads, you're asking for trouble.
- The larger the disk, the better brake performance and modulation. The disadvantage of a larger diameter disk is its higher weight, with different sizes varying by as much as 100 to 200 g. More and more manufacturers offer upgrade kits for larger disks. Both Hayes and Shimano offer kits for (and with) disks up to 203 mm diameter.

2. THE DISK DRAGS

Some disks just do—they're actually designed so that one side of the disk is almost always in contact with one of the pads, and those models should only be used on downhill bikes that aren't often pedaled by the rider. If the disk wasn't meant to drag, you should do a systematic error analysis: Check whether the disk is perfectly flat or wobbles as it turns (replace the disk if there's more than a mm of variation). The wobbling can also be due

to an imprecisely made hub. Periodic rubbing, e.g. only when you pedal forcefully out of the saddle, is often due to use of lightweight construction. Check whether it's the disk that's off or the hub. If it's neither, you probably have a crooked brake cylinder, and here's a list of solutions:

- Paint removal: Thickly applied paint finish on the seating surface for the brake are often the reason for crooked installation of a brake. Carefully scrape off only the paint with a knife blade, otherwise you'll damage the frame or the fork.
- Machining: Special machine tools designed for this application not only remove excess paint, they also align the metal surfaces 100 percent accurate. Since such tools are quite expensive, it's the kind of thing to leave to a well-equipped bike shop.
- What if the seating surfaces are level and the disk rotates perfectly, yet the pads still drag on one side? In that case, your last recourse is the use of shim washers, which are usually included with a disk brake aftermarket installation kit. Make sure you get stainless steel ones in the sizes 6 x 12 x 0.5 mm. If you're a real perfectionist, you can even get them in thicknesses all the way down to 0.1 mm.
- Often it's just a matter of a carelessly installed bike wheel that's responsible for a dragging disk brake. Check every time you install the wheel in the bike to make sure it's seated properly and exactly in the middle, and tighten the quick-release very firmly (install the quick-release so that the quick-release lever is on the side opposite the disk and adjust the thumb nut on the opposite side so that it takes significant force to push the quick-release lever all the way over). Don't try to save weight here, and shy away from aluminum or titanium products because they're not strong enough for this application.
- Never apply the brakes with the wheel removed, because the brake pads would be pushed in against each other and will never return to their proper seating. Always install the plastic plate that's supplied with the brake when the wheel is off the bike. If you forget to use that plate, push the brake pads back in with a screwdriver before installing the wheel.

3. THE BRAKE SQUEALS

- Thoroughly clean the disk. But beware: Don't use a cleaning solvent that may contain traces of mineral oil or solvent, which would be detrimental to the brake's performance. Use only clean water with a drop of e.g. dishwashing liquid or cleaning alcohol. Some swear by 150 grit emery paper because it removes dirt and grease that's penetrated into the outer layer of disk material. Use it in a circular motion in the direction of normal rotation of the disk.
- It's hardly possible to clean gummed-up brake pads. Once they are contaminated, it's best to just replace them entirely.
- Squealing can also be due to an improperly tightened wheel hub. Check the quick-release to make sure it's as tight as can be (install the quick-release so that the quick-release lever is on the side opposite the disk and adjust the thumb nut so that it takes significant force to push the quick-release lever all the way over).
- Sometimes brake squeal is due to insufficient spoke tension. Check spoke tension and tighten the spoke nipples half a turn at a time, working all around the wheel, if they're not tight enough.

"SPONGY" APPLICATION

If the brake feels soft when the lever is pulled in to the point where the pads contact the disk, there's probably air in the system or you may have to replace the brake fluid altogether.

- Bleeding: There are various systems available to help you do this. Most convenient to use seems to be Shimano's Bleeding Kit, which works on every other hydraulic brake on the market as well as Shimano's own version.
- Replace brake liquid: Try a different viscosity when replacing the fluid. For example, Magura Royal Blood is thinner (less viscous) than their regular Magura Blood, and changing to this noble variety should keep that manufacturer's brakes more constant in the way they behave under different temperature conditions.
- Warning: Only use the general type of brake fluid for which the brake's seals were designed—mineral oil (e.g. Shimano and Magura) or DOT brake fluid (e.g. Hayes).

12 BRAKE INSTALLATION, MAINTENANCE, AND ADJUSTMENT

Disk brakes can be installed and adjusted by the averagely competent cyclist—providing you pay attention to the installation dimensions for brake lugs and hub compatibility. It's only a matter of minutes to install V-brakes.

DISK INSTALLATION

Aggressive brake performance in any kind of weather and any situation: that's what disk brakes should provide. On these pages, we'll show you how to install and adjust them so this goal is achieved.

INSTALLATION DIMENSIONS

I.A. INTERNATIONAL STANDARDS

Careful: There are two slightly different disk brake mounting standards: the 1999 and the 2000 versions. They both provide for a distance of 51 mm (2 in.) between the two attachment bolts, whether for the front or the rear. However, the 2000 standard places the disk closer to the frame than the 1999 standard.

IB. The dimension to measure is the one between the inside of the dropout and the inside surface of the disk. 1999 standard:

Front: 13 mm; rear: 16 mm. 2000 standard: front 10.4 mm; rear 15.3 mm. When buying or replacing the hub or the brake, make sure they both conform to the same version of the international standard.

2A, 2B. CALIPER POSITION

Make sure the wheel is inserted all the way. If the disk does not run clear of the brake pads, check whether it's the inside or the outside pad that's rubbing. If the inside pad rubs, use equal numbers of thin shim washers (provided in the brake installation kit, see Fig. 2a) on each mounting position. If the outside pad rubs, remove any excess paint from the mounting bosses. If this doesn't do the trick, have the bike shop machine the lug surface down until the disk runs freely.

Once you install the wheel, the force exerted by the quick-release may disturb this equilibrium again, so check once more and make the same kind of corrections if necessary.

On Haynes disk brakes, loosen the two upper bolts, pull the brake lever and hold it while retightening the bolts (see Fig. 2b). This will cause the brake unit to center perfectly with respect to the disk position.

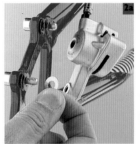

3. BRAKE PAD CLEARANCE

If the brake pads are too far from the disk, this can result in a kind of pumping effect when braking on certain models (e.g. the Magura Luise). If that's the case, first screw both pads in as far as they will go, and then rotate them back until they just clear the disk. This is not necessary on self-adjusting brakes such as those made by Haynes and the Magura Gustav M.

4A, 4B. BLEEDING

Here's how you can tell whether there is air in the system: Even when the lever is pushed past the application point, there's still a spongy feel, and maximum braking requires several applications of the lever before it occurs, and that's when you have to bleed the system.

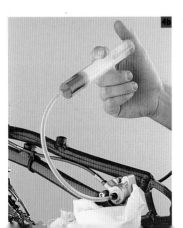

To bleed the system, make sure the bike is placed so that the brake lever is the highest point in the system. Then pump fresh oil in from the lowest point, i.e. the reservoir at the brake caliper. Keep flushing in more oil until you're sure no air bubbles are present. And don't hesitate to "sacrifice" a little more fluid than what you think was just enough.

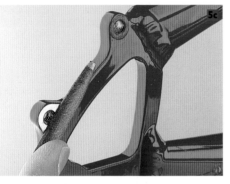

WHAT TO DO WITH SQUEALING DISK BRAKES

The major causes are unwarranted attempts by manufacturers and bikers to make things as light as possible, so that the item's self-resonance frequency is more easily triggered than it is on the more substantial versions used on cars and motorcycles. Here are a few suggestions that may help you eliminate the problem:

1. Roughen up the brake surfaces of the pads with a piece of emery cloth (see Fig. 5a)

2. Apply a thin layer of copper paste to the seats of the brake blocks in the calipers, which will often prevent the propagation of vibrations to the calipers themselves (see Fig. 5b). But be very careful not to get any copper paste in contact with the brake surfaces of the pads.

3. The paint on the contact surface for the caliper mounting bolts can contribute to vibrations. Remove the paint from the contact surfaces with a knife (see Fig. 5c).

4. Clean the brake disk with rubbing alcohol.

5. Place a washer that's slightly larger in diameter under the heads of the caliper mounting bolts.

HYDRAULIC BRAKE FLUIDS

Hydraulic disk brakes work with one of two different types of fluid to transmit the lever force to the brake caliper: Brake fluid or hydraulic oil. They should never be mixed or confused. Check the manufacturer's instruction manual for the type of fluid used and stick with that type only. Especially if you have bikes with different manufacturers' brakes, it's extremely important to check which fluid should be used with the brake you're working on, and banish all other products from the workshop until you've finished the job. Some manufacturers, like Hayes and Magura, offer presumably proprietary fluids for their brakes, but the bottles will reveal to which standard these products are formulated.

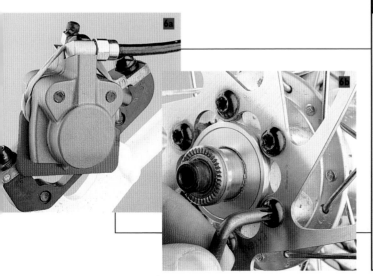

V-BRAKE MAINTENANCE

For a rim brake to stop your mountain bike properly, it has to be properly adjusted. You don't want to have to pull the lever all the way to the handlebars before the brake grabs (see Fig. 1). Find out how to adjust them on these pages.

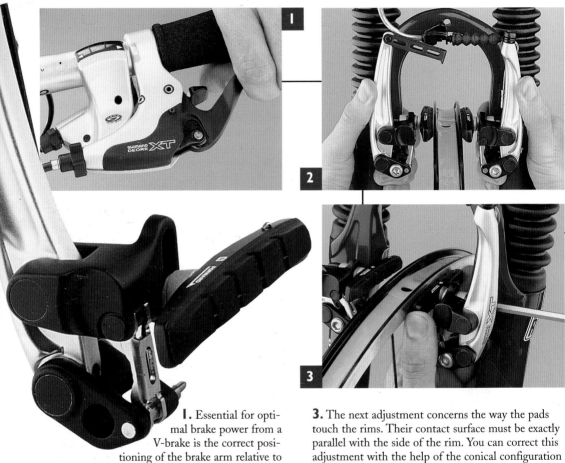

1. Essential for optimal brake power from a V-brake is the correct positioning of the brake arm relative to the rim. They should be perfectly vertically aligned at the point where the brake pad comes in contact with the side of the rim. Since rims come in a wide variety of widths, you'll have to do some work to get the brake pads to protrude just the right distance from the brake arms to achieve this ideal configuration.

2. Use the spacers of different thicknesses provided by the manufacturer, placed over the pad mounting stud between pad and brake arm to achieve this. Use whatever combination of spacers is needed to get the pads to contact the rim when the brake arms are vertically aligned (see Fig. 2).

3. The next adjustment concerns the way the pads touch the rims. Their contact surface must be exactly parallel with the side of the rim. You can correct this adjustment with the help of the conical configuration of the seating for the brake pad stud mounting on the brake arms. Also make sure there is just a tad (one tad equals 1 mm in this case) of clearance between the top of the brake pad and the edge of the rim to prevent the brake pad from eventually creeping into contact with the tire sidewall. Tighten the bolts firmly once the pads are aligned. Squealing can sometimes be prevented by mounting the pads so that the front touches the rim just before the rest of the pad.

4. There's a simple trick that will help optimize the distance between pad and rim once the brake cable is clamped in: First open up the cable adjuster at the

brake lever (see red arrow, Fig. 6) by two or three turns, then pull the cable taut at the brake arm until the brake is activated, and tighten the cable clamp bolt on the brake arm (see Fig. 4). Finally you can turn back the adjuster at the lever until there is about 1 mm between the rim and the brake pad on both sides.

5. Now there's a good chance the brake does not work quite evenly: The brake pad on one side will touch before the other side. On modern V-brakes (in the case of Shimano, starting model year 1999), this feature can be corrected with the help of a tiny (2 mm) Allen bolt on the side of the brake arm just above the pivot point (see Fig. 5). Tighten the screw on the side that lags behind and back off on the other one until the brake pads touch the rim at the same time.

6. The activation point of the brake can be adjusted at the brake levers. Shimano XTR and Deore XT models are equipped with an adjuster that becomes visible when you unhook the cable at the brake and pull the lever in all the way. The cable nipple is seated in a hole that's blocked by means of two wedges (see white arrow, Fig. 6). Once you remove those wedges, the cable nipple can move inward when braking, retarding the application point. On LX brake levers, there are three alternate positions that can be adjusted with a small Allen screw.

Before you make any of these adjustments, first try to get used to the way the V-brake responds as it came from the factory. Once you get used to it, you'll probably find there is no need to make any modifications, unless the brake application point has shifted with use and you want to get it back the way it was originally.

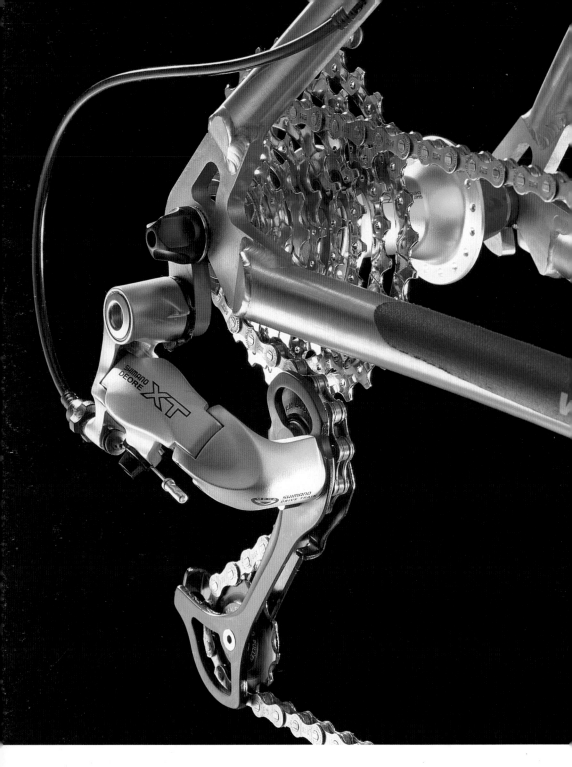

13 GEARING SYSTEM MAINTENANCE AND ADJUSTMENT

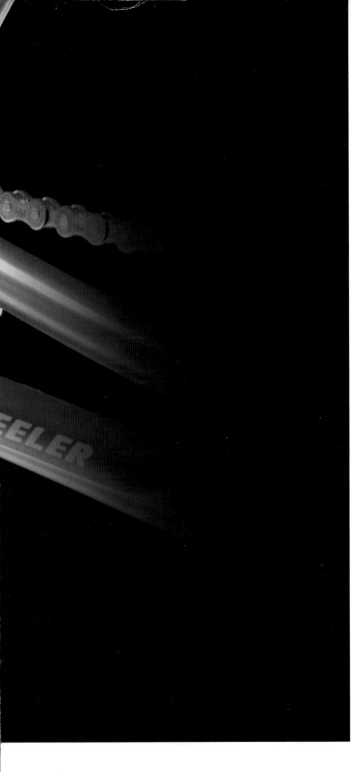

The mountain bike has come a long way: from converted single-speed cruiser to 27-speed rocketship with 3 gears up front and 9 in the back. We'll show you how to adjust and maintain all those gears.

The mountain bike pioneers of the late 1970s were pushing singlespeeds up the hill in order to experience the quick thrill of diving down along the slopes of Mount Tam, relying on gravity and their handling skills. If Shimano (and also initially SunTour) had not taken up the challenge and developed ever-more sophisticated mountain bike components, we would perhaps still be walking up most hills. But thanks to the input of the California pioneers and the engineering skills of the Japanese manufacturers, today's mountain bikes offer the gearing that makes it possible to pedal up almost any slope—and shift with confidence and precision.

Today, Shimano's name is practically synonymous with sophisticated mountain bike technology, especially when it comes to drivetrain components (i.e. cranksets, derailleurs, cog sets, and matching chains). Their hierarchy of component gruppos, in fact, offers a convenient framework for the application categories within the general range of mountain biking. Shimano matches the various components of each gruppo to the same standards in terms of weight vs. durability, accuracy, finish, and adjustability, and in some cases actual dimensioning (and the same holds true for other component makers, even if they don't offer as many complete gruppos).

Consequently, these components can be assured to work optimally well together as long as they come out of the same gruppo, but not necessarily if they're gathered out of several different bins, so to speak. So, if you select individual components to assemble the bike yourself, we recommend you avoid selecting them from categories that are separated by more than one or two levels. To give an example, it's OK to combine XTR with XT or Deore

LX components, but not to combine XTR components with those from much cheaper gruppos like Alivio. That would be like putting a modern Porche engine in an ancient VW bug.

Currently, all Shimano gruppos of Deore and above are available with 9-speed cassettes in the

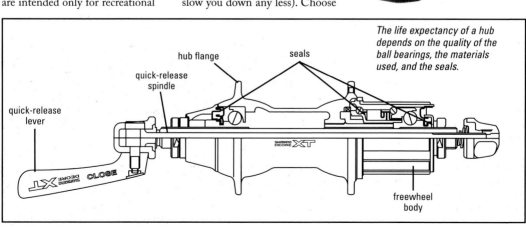

Pretty, smooth, and unfortunately rather pricey: Shimano's XTR Rapid-Fire brake-shift lever combination.

rear, providing theoretically 27-speed gearing (although there is always some overlap). Actually, it looks like 10-speed versions, first introduced on high-end road bike gruppos, may well be on their way for mountain bike use as well. Shimano's cheapest "real" mountain bike gruppo is the Alivio, which is available with "only" 8-speed cassettes and V-brakes—today's true test of off-road competence. Anything cheaper than that, such as Altus and Tourney, are intended only for recreational

riding, which at best includes dirt-path riding. The Deore series is really the benchmark of mountain bike componentry. Even on bikes set up generally with higher-ticket items, you'll frequently find vestiges of the Deore gruppo wherever it's acceptable to pay a slight weight and "looks" penalty without sacrificing performance.

One thing you can't do with impunity is mixing 8-speed and 9-speed components: if you have a 9-speed cassette, make sure you also use 9-speed shifters and a chain designed for 9-speed use to achieve good performance.

In competitive use, the XTR gruppo sets the standard of excellence—minimal weight, sophisticated shifting ease, beautifully finished, and lots of "wow." However, there's no reason to spend that kind of money if you don't have a sponsor to foot the bill. Deore XT, Deore LX, and even plain Deore components won't make you go noticeably slower (or, in the case of brakes, slow you down any less). Choose

the best components you can afford and don't feel tempted to mortgage the home just to keep up with those who can afford the latest and lightest components. As long as you maintain your bike and components well, cheaper components work as least as well as top components that are neglected.

In an analogy with the personal computer market, you can think of Shimano as being something like Microsoft. So where's the Apple equivalent? Perhaps it's SRAM, a U.S. company which bought out the German Sachs company back in 1998 and has

The life expectancy of a hub depends on the quality of the ball bearings, the materials used, and the seals.

quick-release lever

quick-release spindle

hub flange

seals

freewheel body

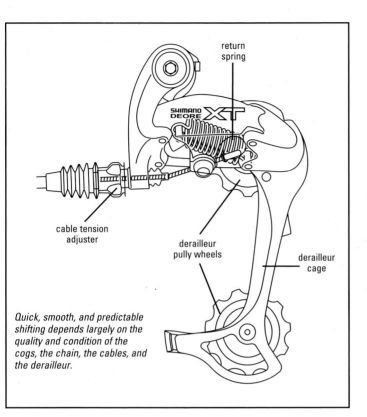

return
spring

SHIMANO DEORE XT

cable tension
adjuster

derailleur
pully wheels

derailleur
cage

*Quick, smooth, and predictable
shifting depends largely on the
quality and condition of the
cogs, the chain, the cables, and
the derailleur.*

since then integrated products from those two lines in a coherent gruppo lineup. So far, they've really only successfully cracked the low-end market, and you'll see their products mainly on bikes sold at places like Sears and K-Mart in the U.S. That's a shame, because their top-rated 9.0 and 7.0 gruppos seem to be worthy contenders with mid-range Shimano components. Until recently, all of SRAM's gruppos used rotating twistrings on the handlebars instead of push-lever controls for gear selection, whereas Shimano only offers twistrings on some of its low-end gruppos.

The choice of shifting method will be the one fundamental decision to make in this regard: If you'd rather turn a twistring to operate the gears, choose a SRAM gruppo, otherwise, stick with Shimano. The arguments for the twistring solution are greater shifting ease (at least in some

riders' opinion) and fewer bits sticking out from the handlebars for a "cleaner" look. Shimano's Rapid Fire shifters, on the other hand, are well-tested and the reason "everybody" uses them isn't just attributable to market dominance: Those things really work very well under all conditions, including rain, sleet, and snow, where SRAM shifters still haven't proven themselves as thoroughly yet.

FINDING OUT WHAT GOES TOGETHER

Shimano drivetrains are of two essentially different designs: Hyperglide and Interglide. The table below shows which components are mutually compatible. Even so, there may be slight deterioration compared to combining only components from the same gruppo.

	IG Cassette	IG Chainrings	HG Cassette	HG Chainrings
IG Chain	YES	YES	YES	LIMITED
HG Chain	LIMITED	NO	YES	YES

REAR DERAILLEUR ADJUSTMENT

Adjusting a derailleur for proper operation is not difficult. We'll explain all you need to know on these pages, regardless whether you have a system with 7, 8, or 9 cogs in the rear.

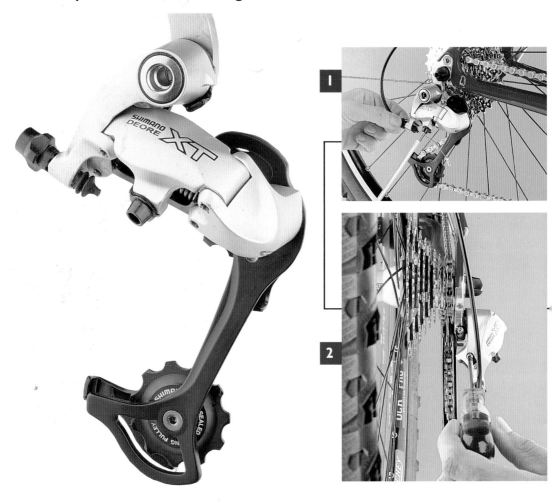

1. Before you start, put your gears in the following initial position: Select the middle chainring in the front, combined with the smallest cog in the rear. Next, undo the cable clamp bolt on the rear derailleur. Then check to make sure that the cable adjusters at the rear derailleur (see Fig. 1) and at the corresponding shifter (see Fig. 6) can be turned both ways by at least 2 full revolutions (if not, turn them until they are in a position where that's possible).

2. Now turn the upper Philips head adjusting screw (for all derailleurs except SRAM's ESP models, where it's the lower screw instead) until the center of the derailleur cage is perfectly lined up with the smallest cog. The easiest way to do this is with the bike raised off the ground on a work stand; then you can turn the cranks and adjust the screw until the chain runs silently over the cog.

3. Check to make sure the right-hand shifter is set for the highest gear. Then pull the cable taut at the derailleur with a pair of pliers and tighten the cable clamp bolt on the rear derailleur. Then carefully shift to the lowest gear, largest cog, with the right-hand shifter. In this position, the center of the cage should line up perfectly with the largest cog. You can use the other Phillips head adjusting screw on the derailleur to limit how far the derailleur cage with the chain can be pushed towards the center of the

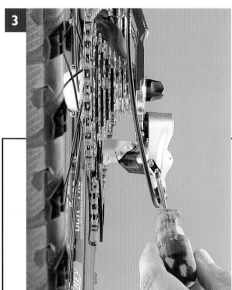

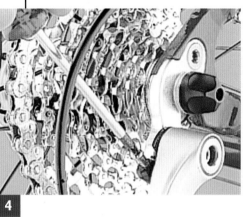

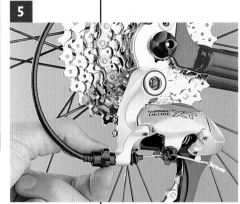

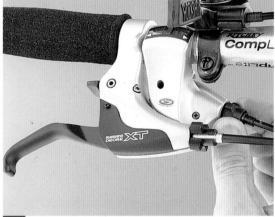

wheel. Careful: The chain can drop off the cog and get enmeshed in the spokes if this screw is not correctly adjusted.

4. If the bike is equipped with a very big cog (30 teeth or more), it can happen that the upper one of the two little pulley wheels contacts that large cog, causing noises. Only in that case do you have to adjust the third Phillips head adjusting screw (the lonely one in the back of the rear derailleur) to modify the rear rerailleur's "angle of dangle" to increase the distance between the pulley wheel and the cog.

5. Now shift up-and-down several times through the entire range of gears, then shift back to the center cog (on 9- and 7-speed systems) or one of the two closest ones (on 8-speed systems), making sure it runs silently. If not, you can adjust the derailleur cable by means of the cable adjuster at the derailleur. Usually it only takes about half a turn.

6. The adjuster at the shifter (see Fig. 6) has the same function as the one at the derailleur. If you find the rear derailleur runs noisily when you're out on a ride, that's the one to use for a quick fix as you continue to ride along. In a case like that, it's usually a matter of screwing the adjuster out (rather than in), because you're compensating for cable stretch.

FRONT DERAILLEUR ADJUSTMENT

Although not used as often as the rear derailleur, the one in front gets to do the hard work, having to deal with the portion of the chain that's under tension due to pedaling force. But adjusting it properly is just as easy as it is for the one in the back.

1. First make sure the front derailleur is in the right position. The inside of the outer cage plate must be 1–2 mm above the top of the teeth of the largest chainring, and the outside of the outer cage plate must be parallel to the chainrings. If necessary, loosen the bolt with which the front derailleur is clamped to the frame, shift it, and retighten. If this does not solve the problem, read on.

2. Shift into a gear that combines the smallest chainring in front with the biggest cog in the rear. Loosen the Allen bolt that holds the shifter cable at the front derailleur (see Fig. 4 or 5). Then adjust the outer one of the two little Phillips head adjusting screws on top (see Fig. 2) to position the inner cage plate so that it barely clears the chain as you turn the cranks with the wheel raised off the ground.

3. Check to make sure that the cable adjuster at the left-hand shifter (see Fig. 6) can be turned both ways by at least 2 full revolutions (if not, turn them until they are in a position where that's possible). Then reinstall the cable at the front derailleur (see Fig. 4 or 5)

4. Shift the chain onto the biggest chainring and

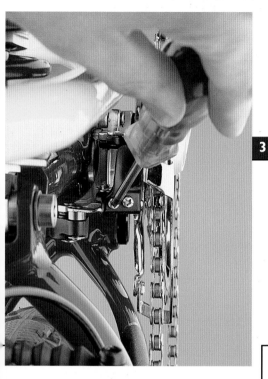

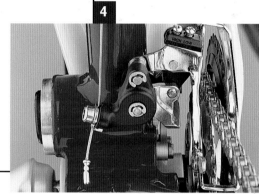

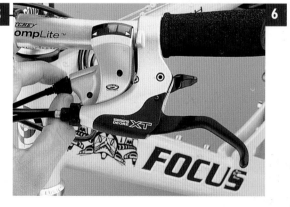

adjust the inner one of the two Phillips head adjuster screws (see Fig. 3) to bring the outer cage plate just far enough so that the chain just clears when you shift the rear derailleur (right-hand shifter) for the chain to engage the smallest cog.

5. Adjust the cable tension with the adjuster at the left-hand shifter (see Fig. 6). To do that, first select the middle chainring, and adjust the cable tension so that the chain runs silently as you shift between the gears in the back. If it turns out to be impossible, accept occasional noise in an extreme gear rather than a position where the chain is shifted beyond the chainring.

6. Experience shows that you're more likely to need the gear that combines the largest cog in the rear with the middle chainring. So if you have to make compromises, that's the gear in which you want the chain to run silently, even if it's at the expense of noise in the gear with the chain running on the smallest cog.

7. With a little practice, you'll be able to fine-tune the front derailleur "on the fly," using the adjuster at the shifter (see Fig. 6). But before you try your luck with that, spend some time with the bike on the work stand, learning the effects of certain adjustments.

14 MAINTENANCE OF CRANKS AND BOTTOM BRACKET

The cranks and the bottom bracket are the mountain bike's most heavily loaded components. This chapter explains everything you need to know to select and install these essential drivetrain components.

The cranks and the bottom bracket bearings lead a stressed-out existence. They're always at work, driven by the rider's pedaling motions, and even when you're not pedaling, your weight is likely to be applying significant forces to these components. During a five-hour ride, the bottom bracket spindle rotates about 20,000 times, and the load keeps being shifted from the left crank to the right one and back again, over and over.

Actually, measurements confirm that the rider can on occasion apply three times his or her body weight to bear on the pedals—that's 240 kg (530 lbs) or so for an average rider, more for heavyweights—on each crank arm. Metalurgical and mechanical experience also confirms that the intermittent nature of this force application increases its destructive effect. So they'd better be made well, and you'd be well advised to keep them in good condition with frequent and painstaking maintenance.

So how do you judge the quality of a crank arm? In essence, it's a matter of materials, design, and quality control. The cold forging process has been proven to be a reliable method of producing strong and durable crank arms. Don't take the word "cold" too literally: It means the metal is hot alright, but not quite so hot that it begins to melt. A chunk of aluminum alloy (or steel for that matter) is pushed into shape over a series of subsequent steps involving high-force presses until the final shape is achieved, after which it's cleaned up a little to remove rough edges and to improve the fit around the axle. Then screw threads are machined in and they're engraved with the manufacturer's name and model designation.

The favored material for cranks (and many other bicycle components) is an aluminum alloy of the designation 7075. This material lends itself both to machining and forging and may be heat treated for greater strength afterwards. Even though some small manufacturers offer very cool looking CNC-machined versions, cold forging is actually the preferred process for these products because it enhances the metal grain structure for greater strength. Steel, though also quite suitable for crank fabrication, is hardly used any more on quality bikes.

In recent years a number of manufacturers (including market leader Shimano), have started making hollow cranks to save weight by means of welding parts together. So far, they've received excellent report cards, but yes, they're expensive (Shimano's current crop of XTR cranksets are produced this way).

More expensive to make are carbon-fiber fabricated cranks, on which the ends are aluminum forgings held together with a hollow section of carbon fiber. Yes, they are lighter, but not yet extensively tested and proven.

As for the way the chainrings are attached to the right-hand crank, things have changed in recent years. Formerly, the right-hand crank had an integral star-shaped array of attachment arms, but on recent incarnations crank and attachment arms have become separated. Traditionally, the attachment array consists of five arms, and while Shimano made its high-end crank attachment with four arms for

a few years, they're now back to five arms—which is rather unfortunate in terms of compatibility of replacement parts.

Now for the chainring sizes. First there's the number of teeth to consider. The traditional mountain bike arrangement is three chainrings in sizes 46/36/26 teeth, but led by SunTour in the early 1990s, compact drive units with 42/32/22 teeth have become the norm. These are typically combined with smaller cogs in the back than the old standard, but that's not the topic of this chapter. What matters more is the location of the bolt holes. With the confusion caused by 4- or 5-point attachments, and compact or standard chainrings, it's a matter of making very sure you measure the existing part carefully before buying a replacement. Or, better yet, take the right-hand crank with you to the shop when buying replacement chainrings.

Traditionally, the cranks have tapered square holes that fit onto matching tapered square ends of the bottom bracket spindle. However, in recent years Shimano has been using a splined configuration instead, which they refer to as "Octagon." first introduced for the XTR series, it's slowly beginning to trickle down and by 2003 had reached all the way down to Alivio. Here too, make sure what you have before ordering fitting replacement parts.

Crank length is virtually standardized at 175 mm, although

they're still available in 170 mm, which is recommended for riders under 170 cm (5 ft. 7 in.). Even shorter crank lengths, like 165 mm still exist but are hard to find and only available for square tapered spindles.

The Octagon splined bottom bracket spindle design was first introduced on Shimano's XTR line of components and has meanwhile trickled down to other gruppos as well. The unit illustrated is a 2002 model year XTR, which is not fully sealed (unlike other and newer models), so it requires more maintenance.

THE BOTTOM BRACKET

The old-fashioned bottom brackets with adjustable ball bearings have been replaced by the new industry standard: sealed bearing units with installation rings that are screwed into the sides of the bottom bracket shell. Units that are self-contained are referred to as cartridge or compact units. Their advantages are ease of installation, no maintenance or adjustment required, and usually very durable.

These cartridge bottom bracket units come in different price, weight, and quality variants with steel or titanium spindles and steel, aluminum, or plastic installation fittings, and in the quality and number of bearings. The highest quality units run on three or even four bearing sets, including roller bearings as well as conventional ball bearings. The idea is to minimize deflection (i.e.

bending) and torsion (i.e. twisting) of the spindle, which itself should be as rigid as possible. That keeps the drivetrain efficient and reduces wear of the individual bearings and other components to a minimum.

Although titanium spindles are lighter than steel ones, they

A proven design: The XT crankset is rugged and will serve you well for many years.

Hollow crankarms minimize weight without sacrificing strength and rigidity.

are not as rigid and there are often problems with the seating surfaces of the cranks. If you care for durability and reliability, this is a bad place to save weight, but if you want to spend extra money, a hollow steel spindle and the best possible bearing arrangement will serve you better than a titanium spindle. Even dual bearings have proven to be very reliable on high-quality bottom brackets such as Shimano's XTR and Deore XT models.

The length of the spindle and the width of the bottom bracket

shell form important criteria when replacing a bottom bracket unit. A shorter spindle will be more rigid than a longer one, and the distance between bearings is determined by the width of the frame's bottom bracket shell. By using so-called low-profile cranks, it has become possible to make shorter, and therefore more rigid, spindles. Whereas 122 mm used to be the typical length, we now often find spindles of either 107 or 113 mm length. Of course, that only works if you use the matching low-profile cranks, otherwise they'll interfere with the bike's chainstays.

The most common dimensions for the width of the frame's bottom bracket

Hollow, welded cranks were first used by Shimano on their XTR model, although other, smaller vendors had similar items before.

Between the model years 1997 and 2003, Shimano used 4-bolt configurations, but starting in 2004 they'll use 5-bolt attachments again.

shell are 68 or 73 mm, and that too will have to be factored in, because you may not be able to use that short spindle unit if the bottom bracket is too wide to accept it.

Another critical dimension is the chain line—the distance from the center of the frame to the center position of the chain when it runs on the middle chainring and the middle cog in the rear, and this is a dimension only the bike shop can easily determine. In short: Check the exact dimensions of the frame, and preferably take it with you to let the bike shop confirm that certain combinations of cranks and bottom brackets will work satisfactorily with your frame before you spend your money on replacements.

As mentioned before, the bottom bracket is a bad place to try saving weight. Just the same, it may be of interest to know that we've found differences ranging all the way from 140 g to 327 g (the latter figure applies to a Shimano Deore LX).

The screw thread in the bottom bracket shell for installation of the bottom bracket unit is pretty much standardized as the English BSA-standard, although, on older bikes, there are still some French and Italian bikes around that are made to different screw-thread specifications.

For the installation details of the cartridge bearing bottom brackets, the Shimano standard has been pretty generally adapted. That means that you'll need only one bottom bracket tool, costing about U.S. $8, to remove, install, or adjust almost any bottom bracket on the market today.

BOTTOM BRACKET AND CRANK INSTALLATION

CRANK REMOVAL

Before you start work on the bottom bracket, you'll have to remove the cranks. Using a long Allen wrench, undo the Allen bolt that holds the crank to the bottom bracket spindle. On most modern cranksets, this will simultaneously pull the crank free from the spindle. If not, remove the bolt, install a crank puller (with the interior part turned back in), and tighten it to push the crank off the spindle.

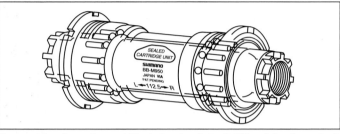

Cross-section of a modern cartridge bottom bracket unit. This unit has four sets of bearings, an inside ball bearing and an outside roller bearing on each side. Also note the width dimension (112.5 mm) and the splined Octagon spindle ends.

CRANK MATERIAL SELECTION

ALUMINUM
Has long been the standard material for mountain bike cranks. Arguments in favor of aluminum include both its low weight and the fact that it can be formed and machined relatively easily. Cheap aluminum cranks are cast, or drop-forged, while high-quality ones are cold forged. After they have been forged, they are machined to install the pedal screw thread, the hole for spindle attachment, and (on the right-hand crank) chainring attachment. The surface is usually anodized for protection, and sometimes a pigment is added to the anodization to give them a different color. Small-scale specialist manufacturers manufacture entire cranks using (digitally controlled) CNC machines.

STEEL
There's nothing wrong with steel as a material to make cranks. The higher specific weight (as compared to aluminum) can be offset by smaller cross-sectional dimensions. It's quite possible (though by no means cheap) to make welded steel cranks with hollow, tubular arms that weigh less than most aluminum cranks and are at least as strong.

CARBON FIBER
This magic material combines highest strength and lowest weight qualities to make superb components in general. When it comes to cranks, though, the shape of the product makes it hard to achieve a competitively priced design. The manufacturing method involves placing layers of fiber mats around a light foam core, which are soaked in a bonding resin. By selectively applying more layers at the most highly stressed area (near the bottom bracket spindle), it's possible to come up with a very strong and light design. Unfortunately, the thin layer of material—though strong in the direction of normal stress—is sensitive to side impact, and the crank may be ruined by getting hit with a small, hard object from the side.

BOTTOM BRACKET INSTALLATION

1. Have the screw thread cut or "chased" (see Fig. 1). Don't try this yourself: It's a job for a bike mechanic and may be unnecessary if you're replacing an existing bottom bracket unit. It will be required on first installation in a new frame. The screw thread on both sides of the bottom bracket shell must be perfectly aligned and perpendicular to its side surfaces.

2. Insert the main unit of the cartridge from the chainring side (i.e. from the right-hand side of the frame, see Fig. 2). Take care not to damage the thread and make sure the screw tread is perfectly aligned with its mate inside the bottom bracket shell. This side has left-hand screw thread, and that means it has to be screwed in counterclockwise. Only screw it in about halfway by hand. If it is very hard to screw it in that far, you may have misaligned the screw threads: Remove it and inspect the thread, then try again. If it doesn't go in smoothly or if it keeps going in misaligned, take it to the bike shop to have the screw thread recut and the unit installed.

3. Modern cartridge bottom brackets are supported from both sides in screw-threaded retainer rings, and these have to be installed accurately on both sides to prevent damage to the bearings. Also screw the second retaining ring in halfway by hand—clockwise this time because this side has a "normal" right-hand screw thread (see Fig. 3). Then tighten the one on the chainring side using the bottom bracket installation tool.

4. Tighten the installation ring on the side opposite the chain (left-hand side) and install the lockring on that side. When using

the bottom bracket installation tool to tighten the installation rings, don't hesitate to use all the leverage the long handle offers to make sure the unit is tightly in place. Also the lock-ring must be installed as tightly as possible (don't be fooled by Fig. 4: use the long handle!).

CRANK INSTALLATION

1. Make sure the square or splined surfaces of crank and bottom bracket spindle are perfectly clean and preferably lightly coated with a very thin film of oil.

2. Carefully align the square or splined surfaces of crank and spindle and place the crank on the spindle by hand as far as it will go (see Fig. 5). Make sure the two cranks are exactly opposite each other.

3. Install any washer that may be provided and then install and tighten the crank attachment bolt with an extra long Allen wrench (or, if you have an older crank with a regular hexagonal nut or bolt, using the special crank tool provided). If there's a separate dustcap, install that too.

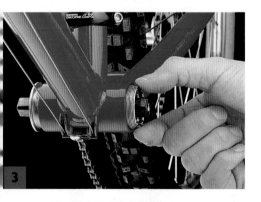

4. Retighten the cranks after an hour's hard use or after about 50 km (35 miles) of easy riding. And pay attention so you notice any creaking sounds, which will be your signal to retighten them again.

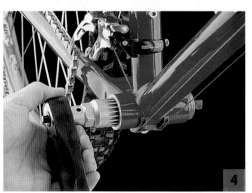

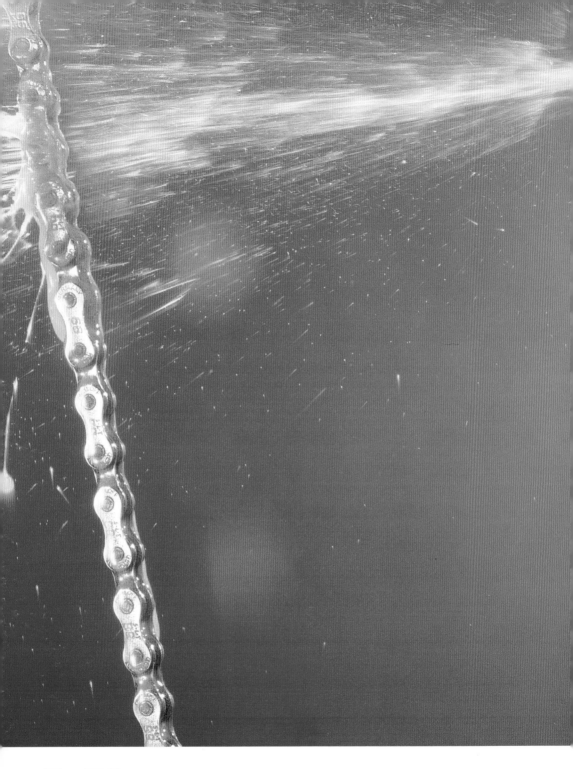

15 CHAIN MAINTENANCE

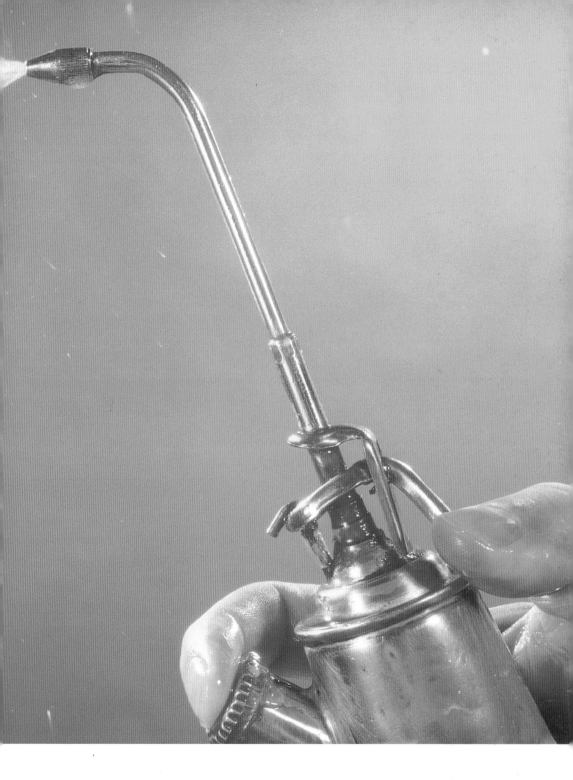

The mountain bike's chain gets a lot of abuse: Transmitting all the power the rider exerts, it also has to jump from cog to cog and from chainring to chainring in response to gear changes. When the chain skips, the gears don't engage properly, and noises come from that end of the bike, it's time to replace the chain.

REPLACING THE CHAIN

You can maximize the chain's life expectancy with frequent checks and maintenance. Also the chainrings and cogs profit from a well-maintained chain. Replace the chain before it's so badly worn that it starts damaging the other drivetrain components.

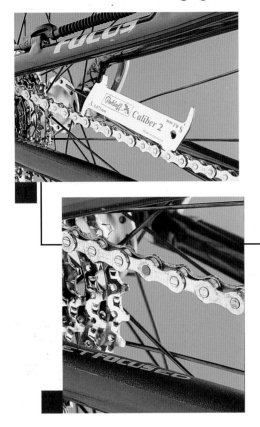

1. There are two possible reasons to remove the chain from the bike: For general cleaning of the drivetrain and to replace it when it's worn out. One way to know when it's time to replace the chain is to measure it for wear (usually after about 2,000 km, or 1,300 miles of use). You can get that done at any bike store, for which they'll use a special chain wear gauge (see Fig. 1). Replacement is due when the second pin on the gauge drops between the rollers. If you don't replace the chain at this point, you risk seriously damaging the chainrings and cogs, which would then also have to be replaced.

2. You'll need a chain tool to remove the chain from the bike. Use the tool to push one of the link pins, or rivets, out (see Fig. 3). But careful: On Shimano HG- and IG-compatible chains, that may not be done at the smooth, black pin (see Fig. 2), because

that's the one last used to replace or install the chain, and removing it would cause excessive deformation. So choose any other one of the link pins. Place the tool over the selected link pin, and turn the handle clockwise to push the pin down. On Shimano chains, push the pin all the way out. On non-Shimano chains, push it so far that the pin still keeps the links connected at one end.

3. For Shimano chains, you'll need a new special link pin (black, just like the one you avoided before, see Fig. 2 and Fig. 5), noting that this pin is longer and gets pushed in with the pointed end first until the part without pointed end is fully engaged; then break off the other part with pliers. On Sachs and other non-Shimano chains, refer to Fig. 6, which shows how far the old pin should remain engaged in the link, and you now have to

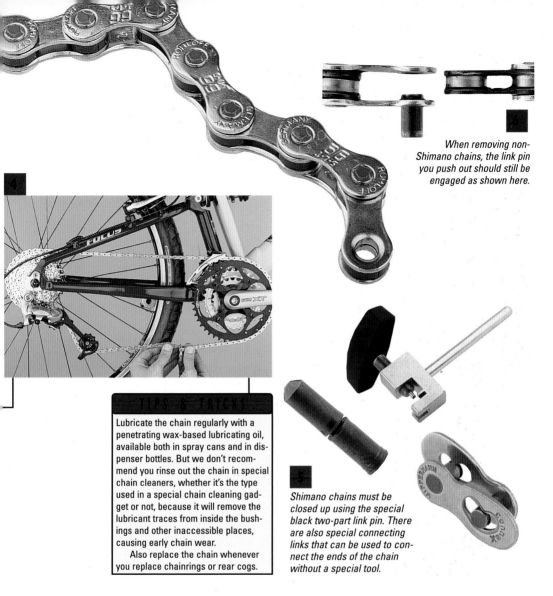

When removing non-Shimano chains, the link pin you push out should still be engaged as shown here.

Shimano chains must be closed up using the special black two-part link pin. There are also special connecting links that can be used to connect the ends of the chain without a special tool.

push that pin back in from the other side (from the bottom in Fig. 6).

4. When installing a new chain, it must first be checked for the right length, and any excess removed using the same method to remove one of the link pins all the way. Place the new chain over the largest chainring and the largest cog (selecting those positions with the shifters) and leaving just a little springiness in the rear derailleur (see Fig. 4). If you make the chain any shorter, there's a risk of doing serious damage to the derailleur if you ever choose that gear when riding the bike. Mark the appropriate link and remove the excess chain length.

5. When installing a Shimano chain, don't forget to use the special link pin illustrated in Fig. 5, which is sold individually in any bike shop. On non-Shimano chains, the pin has to be pushed in until it sticks out equally far on both sides of the chain. Now bend the chain around the connected link pin back and forth and sideways in both directions to make sure it runs smoothly at this point.

6. Beware: None of the conventional chain tools really rivet the chain link pins, which would require the ends of the pin to be spread out to form a "head." That can only be achieved with a professional chain tool, such as the Rohloff Revolver press, which retails at around US $100. Since many bikeshops have a tool like that, you may choose to get the job done there to make sure the connection is really permanent. Alternately, you can use any one of the special connecting links available for most chains, such as the Sachs PowerLink and the Connex; but make sure that it is compatible with the chain on your bike.

16 CLIPLESS PEDAL MAINTENANCE AND ADJUSTMENT

Clipless pedals have taken the mountain bike market by storm. Although many mountain bikers were first skeptical about their application under off-road conditions, they've established themselves as the first choice of most racers and regular riders.

Hardly a serious mountain biker who would forego the distinctive clacking sound associated with getting on the bike and uniting the rider with the bike by engaging the shoes on the clipless pedals. And the introduction in the mid 1990s of reversible pedals that can be ridden with normal shoes on one side, while equipped with clipless engagement systems on the other, has made this method within the reach of beginning riders and touring cyclists as well. A clipless pedal system consists of two parts: The pedal with a spring-loaded clip mechanism, and a matching shoe plate that's attached to the bottom of the shoe.

Before Shimano introduced its SPD standard for mountain bikes for the 1990 model year, clipless pedals, such as those made by Time and Look, had already established a devoted following amongst road racers, while mountain bikers plodded along wearing boots matched up with viciously toothed "bear claw" pedals to keep their feet in place out on the trail. The arguments against their introduction were mainly based on the assumption that the mechanisms would fail in an environment of dirt and mud.

The acronym SPD stands for Shimano Pedaling Dynamics, and even in the first generation of 1990, Shimano managed to solve the two main obstacles to the acceptance for mountain bike use—the need to be able to click into place quickly and securely, even with dirty footwear, and the requirement to allow walking without interference of the shoe plate. And in later versions these features were fine-tuned to the point where there was no longer any reason to hesitate using this technology. The SPD standard has meanwhile been adopted by a number of other manufacturers, who offer SPD-compatible pedals and/or shoes.

On the bike, the advantages of SPD, or any other clipless system for that matter, are threefold: In the first place, the entire force available at the feet is transmitted to the pedals for propulsion; and in the second place, the position of the foot is optimized for maximum pedaling efficiency; finally, no time and effort is wasted while the rider tries to position foot and pedal properly for efficient pedaling.

The optimum position for the foot with respect to the pedal, by the way, is when the ball of the foot (i.e. the first joint of the big toe) is placed directly above the center of the pedal spindle, since that's the point where the foot's pressure is concentrated when a downward force is applied. When adjusting the position of the plate that's attached to the shoe, it should be done in such a way that this situation is realized.

Not only can you push down onto the pedals more effectively with clipless pedals, you can even apply force on the upstroke. Although this may not be a way of increasing long-term cycling efficiency, it can help you get over difficult sections where it's important to keep momentum as much as possible. This action relies on a different set of muscles and joints

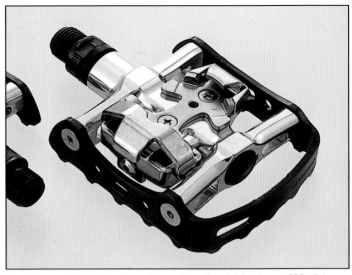

Ideal for mountain bike touring and casual use: A pedal that has an SPD clipless design on one side and a regular pedal surface on the other. This design seems to be on the way out and is being replaced by clipless pedals combined with flat plastic inserts that can be removed. Both types can be used with regular shoes as well as with SPD-cleated footwear.

than the downward pedaling motion, and at times it may be beneficial to transfer some of the work this way, allowing the main leg muscles to recover. The motion of pulling up works best when you get up out of the saddle in what used to be called "honking" in old English cycling books. This technique can be very helpful in overcoming very steep climbs. As you get used to riding this way, you'll find that the forward muscles of the lower leg, which usually get a

free ride when cycling, are called into action. It doesn't hurt to train those muscles this way by practicing the technique of pulling on the pedals.

The clipless pedals also serve the rider well when carrying out such fun activities as jumping with the bike—especially the classical "bunny hop." This kind of jump is awfully hard to master unless your feet are well connected with the pedals, and SPD pedals do just that. Avoid twisting your feet as you jump up, otherwise the pedal may get disengaged, which will make for a failed jump.

Not all mountain bikers really appreciate the very stiff soles used to distribute the load over the entire foot before applying it to the pedal. The main objection is usually that it's hard to walk in those rigid shoes, especially on uneven terrain. If you can't get used to such "proper" SPD-compatible mountain biking shoes, you can try the rather softer versions that are marketed for touring use, which usually have a good profile to prevent slipping on any kind of surface.

SPD-compatible shoe with removable neoprene liner. This is a great shoe for fall and winter riding. The neoprene liner works as an insulator, keeping the feet warm and dry. It can be removed for cleaning.

The choice of make and model of shoe, as long as they're SPD-compatible, is a matter of individual preference. They're now available in a wide variety. Just make sure they fit comfortably—they should fit firmly without allowing movement (up-or-down, back-and-forth, or sideways) of the foot in the shoe. On the other

ting). Some of these foul-weather shoes, and special models for mountain touring, are equipped with removable neoprene liners. This material forms an excellent insulator as well as a moisture barrier (ask any diver, surfer, or windsurfer who uses a wetsuit), thus maintaining the feet comfortably warm in cold and/or wet weather.

A minor detail that bears attention is the lacing of cycling shoes. They should be tightened evenly without squeezing the foot too tightly anywhere. Then it's important to make sure the shoe laces don't stick out so much that the one on the right foot could get caught in the chain near the front derailleur, possibly causing a fall. A nice solution is shoes that close with Velcro straps instead of conventional laces, or alternately shoes with laces that are covered with a Velcro flap. These can even be readjusted without getting off the bike, something many experienced mountain bikers find necessary from time to time.

One of the advantages of SPD-compatible footwear is that it can initially be used without clipless pedals if you're a beginning rider whose confidence isn't quite up to riding in unison with the bike yet. Until you've reached the required level of confidence, simply wear the

More for racing than for getting off and on the bike in difficult terrain: High-end Shimano shoes for use with SPD clipless pedals. With their Velcro and buckle closure, they are comfortable and there's no risk of shoelaces being caught in the drivetrain, as was often the case on older models.

hand, they shouldn't pinch the feet either, because the last thing you want to do is to cut off circulation in the foot, a phenomenon that will be quickly noticed, especially in cold weather.

If the shoe fits so loosely that the foot can slide around inside, you're not only losing efficiency, you're also likely to incur injuries in the form of blisters, which will make pedaling even harder. Relatively high-cut footwear, at least ankle height, is best suited for longer rides, especially if significant sections will have to be taken on foot. These provide a firmer hold, without having to be so tight that they cut off circulation.

Even special models for use in wet terrain have been introduced, and if your bike shop doesn't stock them, you should be able to have them special-ordered (once you establish for sure with another model by the same manufacturer what size you should be get-

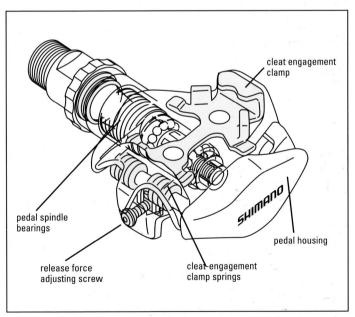

The guts of a clipless pedal exposed: Similar to a modern ski binding, there is a set of spring-loaded clamps that clamp around the cleat, which is mounted on the bottom of the shoe. An angular displacement of the shoe with respect to the pedal releases the mechanism. The release force is determined by the preload of the springs, which can be adjusted by means of the two adjuster screws (in the front and rear of the pedal).

For riders who don't want to entrust their life to a technology that fixes their feet seemingly permanently to the pedals, there are several options available. The first one would be to use Shimano's (or similar) entry-level pedals that click on one side and not on the other. These designs allow you to disengage easily without losing control over the pedals, as would be the case with full-blown clipless designs. The second option, which seems to be edging out the former in Shimano's product line-up, is to choose pedals with "pop-up" clipless mechanisms recessed inside a (rather big) conventional looking pedal. Clicking into position on this latter type of pedal is particularly easy, because the pedal is designed so that it is always positioned for easy entry.

Even on SPD pedals, the beginner's greatest fear of being locked into the pedals without an escape option is highly exaggerated. There is a choice of two different shoe plates, one of which

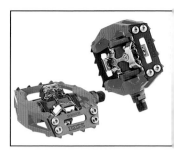

Clipless pedals with rotating pedal plate assure a large contact area and facilitate pedal engagement.

makes both engagement and disengagement quite easy.

Finally, on this subject, one more suggestion for clipless beginners: At first adjust the release force setting of the pedal mechanism for a low force. Practice on quiet paths or empty terrain for some time before you go out into rougher terrain. As you gain confidence, tighten them up in gradual steps until you set them for a relatively high release force after a few months' riding.

Clipless pedals make it much easier to get the bike off the ground.

same shoes without having the shoe plates installed. Then get the plates installed and start using the clipless pedals once your confidence level has increased.

Whatever you do, we advise against riding in conventional tennis shoes. In the first place, they have soles that are far too flexible for comfortable cycling (or, for that matter, even for walking in rough terrain). In the second place, dealing with their long shoe laces makes them a potential safety risk. One manufacturer claims to have carried out tests which indicate that you can only bring 47 percent of maximum force to bear on the pedals when wearing tennis shoes, and in difficult terrain you really want to be able to apply 100 percent, so wasting 63 percent won't get you very far.

Use a 3 mm Allen wrench to adjust the release force spring tension. Start off with a low force setting and increase tension as you gain confidence. Use the same settings on both pedals, and at both sides of each pedal.

INSTALLING PEDAL CLEATS

To use clipless pedals, you'll have to first install the cleats on your SPD-compatible cycling shoes and adjust them correctly.

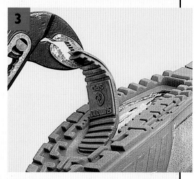

1. Many shoes have a removable section in the sole that covers up the cleat mounting holes. Cut around the contour of this area with a sharp knife (see Fig. 1).

2. Now you can use a screwdriver to lift the cover patch you just outlined. It may be quite hard to remove because it's glued on the main sole plate of the shoe (see Fig. 2).

3. Remove the cover patch with a pair of pliers (see Fig. 3). If it's still attached to the main portion of the sole in some points, make a clean cut with the knife first, so you don't accidentally pull off more than just the patch of the sole.

4. On many types of shoes, you'll have to remove the inner sole, which will reveal the two slots for installation of the cleat. Place the slotted spacer piece that's supplied with the cleat in the recess (see Fig. 4) and cover it with the plate with two screw holes for attaching the cleat with bolts. Hold the plates in place by hand and reinstall the inner sole (sometimes with an intermediate cover piece, if supplied—see Fig. 6)

5. Now you can intall the cleats from the outside through the sole into the screw-threaded holes. The pointed end of the cleat has to point forward toward the toe area of the shoe. Don't forget to install a washer under each Allen bolt. The slotted configuration allows enough up-and-down movement to get

them at the exact point and angle that's comfortable (see Fig. 5). Don't tighten the bolts too vigorously, so it will be possible to shift the location and orientation of the cleat for fine-tuning. The optimum position of the cleat would be centered about the center of the ball of the foot. First determine that point in the shoe and mark it with a felt-tip pen on the sole (also see next page). Fine-tuning is done after some use, preferably in a safe area if you're new to the use of clipless pedals. Start off with the basic position, and then experiment a little by moving it back-and-forth a little, and under slightly different angles, until you feel confident you've reached the optimally comfortable mounting position.

6. Use the patch that is supplied with the cleat to cover the hole in the inside of the sole (see Fig. 6), and we recommend you also cover it all with a patch of duct tape before replacing the inner sole to provide better weather protection.

PEDAL MAINTENANCE

Pedals don't have an easy time: They're always getting kicked around. Learn here how to keep them in top condition with simple maintenance. Also covered are adjustments and shoe plate installation.

1a-c
SPINDLE REMOVAL

Check weather your pedal has a grey splined plastic nut between the pedal housing and the thread stub that screws into the crank. If that's the case, you'll be able to remove the entire spindle cartridge. Shimano pedals of this type (e.g. PD-M 747 or 646)

are supplied with the necessary tool, or you can buy a separate wrench at a bike shop. The same method also applies to many other quality pedals.

Insert the tool over the screw thread and push it down as far as it will go around the splines on the plastic nut (see Fig. 1a). Holding the pedal housing with one hand, rotate the tool with a 35 mm open-ended wrench (see Fig. 1b; you can also use an adjustable wrench). Unscrew the cartridge from the pedal housing by turning counterclockwise for the left-hand pedal, clockwise for the right-hand pedal. If in doubt, watch for the "Tighten" arrows engraved in the plastic—so you'll be turning in the opposite direction to undo them.

There is a sound technical reason for using different thread orientations on the left and right pedals: Due to the high force applied to the pedals, the screw threads holding them in place would tend to get unscrewed if the wrong orientation were used.

If the plastic nut turns out to be too tight, even after you make sure once more you're turning them in the right direction, you can carefully clamp the pedal housing in a vice with soft plastic protector angles in place. After the long threaded portion is disengaged, you can remove the spindle cartridge from the pedal housing (see Fig. 1c).

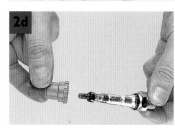

2a-d
BEARING DISASSEMBLY

The axle, or spindle, unit comprises two ball bearings—one at the very end hidden behind the locknut (see Fig. 2a and 2b), and one still invisible inside the short steel sleeve. Remove the locknut with a 7 mm wrench (and, in case the cone underneath turns with it, holding it in place with a 10 mm wrench). Note: Always keep a clean cloth under the pedal as you disassemble the bearings to catch the loose bearing balls.

Under the cone, you'll find 12 small bearing balls (see Fig. 2b). Pull off the steel sleeve, exposing the other bearing (see Fig. 2c). The bearing cup for this bearing rests at the end of the grey plastic sleeve. Once you remove the bearing balls, that sleeve can be removed as well.

Clean all parts, inspect them and replace anything damaged or worn (we suggest you replace the ball bearings by new ones, even if you can't detect damage). Fill the bearing surfaces with bearing grease prior to reassembly and place the bearing balls in this bed of grease. First screw the little cone on the end to hold the bearings together, then hold it with the 10 mm wrench and tighten the locknut. Finally screw the unit back into the pedal housing.

3a
SEALED BEARING UNITS

We don't recommend disassembling pedals on which there is no grey plastic splined nut between the housing and the screw-thread stub as described before. That's because pedals of that type have a cartridge-type spindle with integrated sealed bearing units. (e.g. Shimano PD-M 535). Although you can reach the outer bearing after you remove the outer dust cap, it'll be really difficult to open for maintenance work. And if you manage to disassemble the unit with the help of a set of open-ended wrenches, you'll have to deal with an avalanche of little bearing balls, which are almost impossible to reinstall properly.

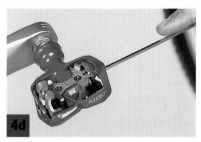

4a-d
CLEAT INSTALLATION

Modern mountain biking shoes almost always come with screw-threaded holes for the installation of SPD-type cleats (or the equivalent Ritchie standard, for which pedals are also readily available). To assure efficiency in pedaling, determine the exact location for the cleat. The ball of the foot must be located directly over the pedal spindle. You'll need a helper to fix this point.

Let your helper check the position of the foot over the pedal for the correct location of the cleat, marking it with a felt-tip pen at the side of the sole (see Fig. 4b). The two cleat installation bolts should coincide with an imaginary line drawn along the sole from this point. This only determines the pressure point

positions for the cleat, without having determined the angular orientation of the cleat. That will be a matter of trial and error. First tighten the bolts with the cleat perpendicular to the line through the two longitudinal slots. Do a test ride, and make any corrections that may be needed until the shoe position feels comfortable (see Fig. 4b), then tighten the screws properly (see Fig. 4c).

Finally, the release force has to be adjusted with a 3 mm Allen wrench to tighten or loosen the pedal spring tension (see Fig. 4d), which must be done separately for both sides of the pedal. Note: When new, the spring tension is set to a the minimum force. Don't loosen it, because the screw will fall out.

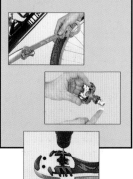

17 WORKING ON THE WHEELS

Strength, reliability, and lightness are the criteria for good mountain bike wheels. All that is reflected in the price. All the more reason to keep those wheels in top condition, so they'll last as long as the bike.

The choice of wheels shows a mountain biker's personal philosophy. Some are so obsessed with weight savings that they're prepared to spend almost any amount of money on a pair of the finest. Others look for strong and rugged, and some get the cheapest wheels they think they can get by with. Whatever type of wheels is installed on your bike, it's worthwhile understanding their construction and function well enough to maintain them correctly for maximum reliability. Because if the wheels give out on a ride, you have little choice but to call it a day.

If it's time to replace your wheels, or when building up a bike with your own choice of components, there are two ways of dealing with the choice of wheels: Either you select hub, rim, and spokes for assembly at the bike shop (or, with the advice in a good wheel-building manual, to do that job yourself), or you buy a complete wheel "off the shelf." A number of specialist manufacturers now offer complete wheels, and that includes major manufacturers like Shimano and Mavic, as well as smaller and more specialized wheel builders like Spinergy, Rolff, and tune (with a lower case t).

The advantage of the second approach is that these manufacturers have the insider information to be able to select components that are perfectly matched to each other, allowing them to squeeze every ounce of performance out of them. They won't be cheap though, and it's not unusual to find a mountain bike on which the set of wheels represents half the total value of the bike.

Many of these manufacturers go for light, and we've tested sets of wheels that weighed as little as 1,330 grams for a complete set of front and rear wheel (a standard wheel set typically weighs up to twice as much). And for good reason: The weight (or expressed scientifically more correctly, the mass) of large rotating parts is the most critical part of a bicycle's weight with respect to overall performance. The old, though highly exaggerated, saying was "an ounce on the wheels is worth a pound on the frame." Well, in fact it's more like an ounce on the wheels is worth about 2 ounces on the frame, but even so, the difference is remarkably noticeable in a sport where you're always working so close to the margin of performance that the smallest improvement is immediately obvious.

The frequently voiced opinion that carbon-fiber wheels are both lighter and more rigid than conventional spoked wheels with aluminum rims does not always hold true, as we were able to demonstrate with our tests on a custom-built test rig. Although carbon wheels, like those made by Spinergy and Zipp, ranged amongst the stiffest, they were demonstrated to be no lighter than conventional wheels of the same stiffness. Rather than being stiffer than equally heavy conventional wheels, they were just more expensive—by a factor of two or more. Our tests also confirmed that, although it's the overall weight that matters most, the distribution of weight over the wheel as a whole is next in importance. So it's more important to save weight on the tires than on the rim, which in turn is more important than weight saved on the spokes, and least important to save it on the hub. The message here is that it doesn't make much sense to save weight on the wheels unless you also install the lightest tires compatible with the terrain.

If you're buying new rims, consider that on the one hand the rim is a load-bearing part of the bike, but it's also part of the mechanical system for braking the

bike (unless you use disk brakes). Especially in wet weather and muddy terrain, rim wear as a result of braking is a significant consideration. That's why bikes with V-brakes should have rims with plenty of material on the sides. As for carbon fiber rims, which are more wear resistant, they unfortunately don't offer the same quality of braking surface in wet weather.

On a spoked wheel, strong rims are an essential criterion for durability and safety. Lightweight rims that get out of true perform poorly, and if they get worn

Carbon-fiber wheels cost a lot of money and are sought after for their "techno-look." They don't have any advantages over conventional spoked wheels of equal weight. Note how an aluminum rim is embedded in the carbon-fiber structure of the wheel. True, they don't need maintenance, but the downside is that you'll have to discard the entire wheel if it does get damaged.

down too much due to braking, they pose a serious safety threat—they can literally collapse on a steep descent. You want wheels that don't have to be trued frequently but hold up well under normal conditions. The width holds up best in use is 23 to 26 mm, and the wider rims should be used only with the widest tires. A light rider without too aggressive a riding style can make do with rims as narrow as 20 mm—

but not for tires that are more than 2.0 in. wide, because they may literally roll off the rims in corners if they're inflated to a rather low pressure (less than 45 psi, or 3 bar).

At the upper end of the price-and-quality spectrum range aluminum rims with ceramic braking surfaces. These are extremely hard-wearing, while getting the most out of your V-brakes' performance potential as long as the special matching brake pads are used.

The best spokes to use are double butted steel spokes (the thinner section between the butts provides the flexibility needed to minimize spoke breakages, while the thicker sections provide the material where it's most needed for strength). You can spend a lot more money on titanium spokes or "aerodynamic" narrow-profile spokes, but their weight savings potential is in no proportion to their higher price.

Whether to use wheels with 32 or 36 spokes has been largely

answered for you: 32 spokes has become the industry standard, with even fewer spokes on many special lightweight wheels, and 28 spokes seem to work out fine for most kinds of off-road use.

The rims should be of the now-common hollow chamber cross-section, which are significantly stronger than cheap U-shaped cross-section rims. Their stability is also maxi-

In recent years, several manufacturers have introduced tubeless tires for mountain bike use, requiring special rims, which are also much harder to spoke in than conventional ones, but they are at least also suitable for conventional tires with separate inner tubes, leaving more options open when you have a tire problem.

All of the above was really addressed to the "average" mountain

disk-brake wheels on the market, and you're well advised to select those. It saves you the trouble of finding out with trial and error which hubs, rims, spokes, etc, stand up to the abuse sudden stops subject them to.

Mountain bike wheels must be strong and rigid; otherwise, they will not stand up to the ravages of off-road use. To make a wheel both strong and light is not impossible, but it costs a lot more.

mized by greater width and depth in profile. The greater width works to counter the tendency to get out of true, while greater depth tends to keep them round better. In mountain biking, there's little to be gained from the use of so-called Aero rims, which have an extremely deep V-profile: They're just harder to spoke in.

Most rims have ferrules—reinforcing bushes—to reinforce the spoke holes, and that's preferable over unreinforced spoke holes. If these ferrules are made of stainless steel, instead of e.g. aluminum, you'll find it much easier to turn the spoke nipples when truing the wheel. A drop of oil under the nipple will have a similar effect on rims without stainless steel ferrules.

biker, whose primary conditions are best described as cross-country use. Freeriders and downhillers need their wheels to be stronger and, in consequence, heavier. For that kind of use, you may want to choose wider rims (up to 30 mm), 36 spokes, and really wide tires of 2.35 in. or more. And, of course, in this category, you may want to use disk brakes, which require special hubs.

Disk brakes also increase the demands placed on the wheel's structure. There are specially built

The rims for wheels designed for use with disk brakes can be built wider and shallower. Due to the torque applied to the wheel when braking the disk, they get to endure very high forces when braking.

WHEEL TRUING

Keeping your mountain bike's wheels running true, without wobbling side-to-side or up-and-down as they rotate, is easy enough to do for the average home mechanic.

1. The spokes on either side of the wheel pull the rim in their respective direction with a certain force. The balance between these forces from both sides is what provides the stability, keeping the wheel round and centered. The force on each spoke can be increased or decreased by tightening or loosening the nipple with which it is held in the rim. If not enough force is applied in one area, the rim will move in the opposite direction, making the wheel "out of true." To true the wheel again, all you need do is increase the force on the spoke that doesn't exert enough force.

Minor deviations, in the range of up to 3 mm (⅛ in.) can be corrected using the brake as a centering guide (assuming the bike has V-brakes, see Fig. 1). You don't even have to remove the tire for this work. For major wheel truing work, it's better to buy a truing stand (see Fig. 2 and 3). One tool you will need either way is a spoke wrench, making sure it's the exact size for the nipples on your bike.

First rotate the wheel slowly, watching the distance between the rim and the brake pads attentively to see which section seems to move over too close to one side or the other as the wheel rotates. In the example of Fig. 1, the rim is over too far to the left in the location shown. Establish how many spokes lie in the part of the wheel that's too far to the left, and mark the first and last affected spoke. Starting at a spoke halfway between these points, tighten only the spokes on the opposite side from the wobble by ½ turn. Working toward the marked spokes on both ends of the wobble, gradually

decrease the amount of tightening per spoke.

Check to what extent this has improved the situation, and continue if needed, in very small increments of about ¼ turn at a time. Carefully watch the wheel at the brake pads as you rotate it after each round of tightening and loosening.

2. A truing stand allows you to do the entire job more easily, and you can correct the wheel for bigger deviations with more accuracy. Truing stands have guides for

both lateral deviation and radial deviation. Install the wheel in the truing stand without the tire. Rotate the wheel and check how it wobbles relative to the gauges for lateral trueness (see Fig. 2). Note that the wheel in the illustration is pulled too far over to the left. Now tighten the spokes on the right-hand side. Only if the deviation exceeds 3 mm will it be necessary to loosen the ones on the left-hand side by as much as you tighten its neighbors on the right-hand side. Proceed as described in step 1 for truing without the truing stand until the wheel runs true, i.e. without wobbling sideways.

3. Also check the roundness of the wheel for radial deviation, which will show as a changing distance between the outside of the rim and the radial truing

gauge (see Fig. 3). To correct for this type of deviation, tighten all spokes (i.e. those on the left and on the right) in the area where the rim scrapes on the gauge; loosen the ones in the area that seems to form a low spot on the circumference of the rim. Also in this case, make the biggest correction in the center of the affected area, gradually decreasing to the edges. Start off with half a turn in the middle, decreasing to ¼ turn towards the ends, and work in smaller intervals of ¼ as you get closer to perfection.

After you've corrected the wheel for radial true, check the lateral true once more, and make any corrections that may be needed.

18 HEADSET MAINTENANCE AND INSTALLATION

Perhaps the most unobtrusive component on your mountain bike, the headset is what determines the accuracy and ease of steering system, both when cornering and when going straight. Don't neglect that important part of the steering system.

odern cars and motorcycles rarely suffer breakdowns caused by worn steering bearings. The right choice of materials and dimensions can take care of that. On the mountain bike, it's a different matter. The quest for the lightest possible weight in all components runs counter to the need for a solid and reliable set of bearings there where the bike keeps being hammered most. Unlike most other bearings on the bike, those of the headset don't rotate much but take a lot of impact in axial direction, which is the bane of all bearing designers.

Just the same, mountain bike headset technology has come a long way. Unlike the early mountain bike pioneers, who had to make do with a technology designed for cycling on the road, applied in an environment of hard knocks, today's mountain bike headsets can handle a lot of abuse—assuming the right headset is selected for the kind of use to which the bike will be exposed.

Even within the realm of mountain bike use, vastly different demands can be made of the headset. Easy off-road touring may be possible with any kind of headset, and the use of suspension forks on almost every mountain bike these days makes it even easier. Freeride, downhill, and other extreme performances, on the other hand, call for a headset of the greatest possible strength and durability. And to think what a large disk brake can do when you throw out your anchor to stop a downhill racer makes you wonder how any headset can stand up under such conditions.

The first step towards mountain bike headset improvement dates back to the late 1980s, when Gary Fisher introduced his Evolution design oversize headset. Instead of the standard 1 in. diameter fork steerer tube with matching bearings, this standard called for a much larger diameter of 1¼ in., which proved to stabilize the front of the bike significantly.

The next major improvement was the introduction of the threadless headset by DiaCompe. Named AHeadset, this quickly became the standard for moun-

Even given a particular design, the quality and accuracy of the bearing is what determines the quality and durability of the headset. The type of bearings required are referred to as axial ball bearings (or in some instances roller bearings), and they may either be of the man-

to their bearing surfaces, which led so many older headsets to an early demise.

A problem with special headsets, i.e. those that don't adhere to DiaCompe's AHeadset standard in every detail, may be availability of spares: Before you choose such a headset for your bike, make sure you know how to obtain spare bearings and other "consumables," so you don't get stuck with an irreparable problem on your hands when the headset lets you down eventually. Whatever the use you have in mind, please steer away from lightweight versions—the headset is far too critical a bearing to try to shave off an ounce or so.

AXIAL-RADIAL BEARINGS

DIN-STANDARD BEARING: Industrial standard for bicycle headsets. The fully enclosed bearing cartridges satisfy all requirements of a superior headset bearing. Pressed into bearing cups, they'll withstand almost any kind of abuse, and their seals obviate the need for frequent maintenance.

SHIMANO CARTRIDGE: An improved version of the familiar cup-and-cone headset bearing design. As is the case for DIN standard bearings, the bearing races are combined into pre-assembled units. Due to their slightly inferior seals and poorer bearing race finish, these bearings are not quite as durable and smooth-running as those made to the DIN standard.

CUP-AND-CONE BEARING: Cheaper to manufacture, this is the conventional threaded headset used on low-end bikes. The bearing balls are contained in retainer rings held in bearing cups, which are pressed into the frame's head tube. This type does not hold up in off-road service as well as the other types of headsets.

---

tain bike use, banishing the old threaded headset design almost completely from the mountain bike scene. These headsets are available for several steering tube diamters: 1 in, 1⅛, and 1¼ in. (and yes, bigger is better, but of course headset, head tube, and steerer tube must match). Unlike the old cup-and-cone bearing headset, they fit around a smooth end of the steerer tube, and the handlebar stem is clamped around the steerer tube, with a bolt on top to adjust the tension on the bearing.

Many other manufacturers have long since adopted this standard, or variations on the same general theme, for which they presumably pay Dia-Compe a handsome royalty for each unit sold (and, of course, encouraging others to search for even better designs). With the AHeadset patent running out of steam (patent protection is valid for only 17 years), even Dia-Compe themselves are working on different designs to replace it.

ufacturer's own design or they may be selected from the standardized bearings available to the trade. Such bearings can be made out of extremely hard materials, which are practically impervious to the hammering effect of shocks perpendicular

Another important design criterion with respect to durability is the quality of the seals: In mountain bike use, you don't want water and dirt to penetrate this critical bearing. Standard industrial bearings for this use are protected

THREADLESS HEADSET CLAMP NUTS

The "star-fangled nut" is the original: It is a double spring element connected with a threaded ferrule that serves as an anchor nut to hold the stem bolt on a threadless (i.e. AHeadset type) headset with the function of adjusting the headset (top). Although a little difficult to install, it holds remarkably tightly once in position. A version that's easier to install and can be reused is the rubber clamp nut (center). The most luxurious version is the aluminum clamp nut shown at the bottom, and these are just as easy to install and remove.

HEADSET DIMENSIONS

	1 in.	1⅛ in.	1¼ in.
Steerer tube outside dia.	25.4 mm	28.6 mm	31.8 mm
Fork race (JIS) dia.	26.4/27.0 mm	30.0 mm	33.0 mm
Bearing cup dia.	30.2 mm	34.2 mm	37.0 mm
Steerer tube inside dia.	22.2/19.0 mm	25.4/24.9 mm	28.6 mm

This is one of the finest headsets around. Very expensive, and you can probably find a cheaper one that will serve you as well.

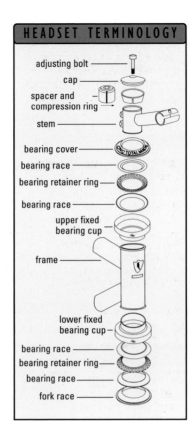

- adjusting bolt
- cap
- spacer and compression ring
- stem
- bearing cover
- bearing race
- bearing retainer ring
- bearing race
- upper fixed bearing cup
- frame
- lower fixed bearing cup
- bearing race
- bearing retainer ring
- bearing race
- fork race

by precisely fitting seals made of a flexible and durable plastic material. Especially bearings without such tightly fitting seals should be inspected at least

TIPS & TRICKS

You should check your bike's headset before every off-road trip. It only takes a few seconds and is well worth the effort, because you can ruin a headset by riding the bike once the headset is no longer properly adjusted. And if you find it wanting, adjust it right away to avoid serious damage.

twice annually and repacked with bearing grease before they are re-assembled. If you can detect the bearing balls from the outside, you're looking at an inadequate headset—reason enough to reject a bike so equipped.

If you want to replace the existing headset by a new one, or if you are equipping a bare frame with your own choice of components, it is recommended to have the bike shop install the headset bearing cups. That's because there may be traces of paint or other materials interfering with the smooth installation: The bike shop is equipped to clean up the seating surfaces and assure a correct fit. The ideal method is to have the top and bottom of the head tube and the top of the fork crown machined perfectly level, which assures the bearings of the new headset will be perfectly

aligned. Once installed accurately like this, the maintenance of most modern sealed headsets will be limited to a single inspection once a year.

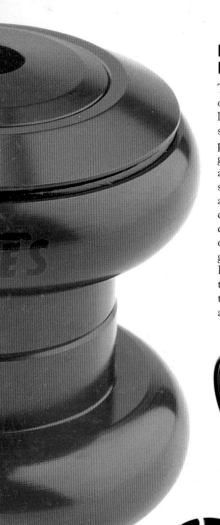

HEADSET MAINTENANCE

The first and most important rule of headset maintenance is not to let things get out of hand. As soon as you notice the slightest problem, don't wait, hoping it will go away, but stop and fix it right away. Left unchecked, even a slight looseness of the bearing, or a little dirt inside, warrants immediate action. It's amazing how quickly a headset can be ruined otherwise. The scenario for things getting out of control is like this: First you notice the steering getting a little looser. Shortly after that, it gets a little unpredictable and it's not so easy any more to steer an exact course.

Finally you experience something like "indexed" steering: It can be steered only in distinct steps, but never exactly the way you want it to go. Avoid that scenario by acting early.

Particularly sensitive are conventional bicycle-type threaded headsets (the type that was used on early mountain bikes before the AHeadset was introduced). After all, those bearings are really not designed to take the abuse of off-road riding. If you have a bike with this kind of headset, our advise is to replace the fork, the headset, and the handlebar stem by a modern design—a good time to finally upgrade to a suspension fork.

You may not have to do frequent maintenance on your headset once you've got a modern version installed, but we still recommend routine checks, perhaps even after every long, hard ride in demanding terrain. Here are the four steps of routine headset maintenance.

A threadless headset with sealed machine bearing units. Although very durable, it shouldn't be neglected either.

BEARING CHECK

Here's a quick and easy way to check your headset bearings to make sure it's not loose: Hold the bike by the handlebars and pull the front brake lever (usually the left-hand lever), then try to push the bike forward and backward by hand, while feeling for movement at the point where the bottom headset, the frame, and the fork crown come together. If you notice any movement, it's a sign that the bearings are not tightly adjusted any more. Don't wait: Adjust it immediately, even if the movement is ever so slight.

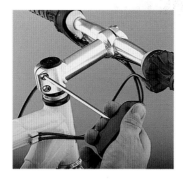

ADJUSTING A THREADED HEADSET

To adjust the conventional threaded headset, you'll need special, large open-ended wrenches to match the locknut and upper bearing cup dimensions (usually 32 mm for 1 in., 36 mm for 1⅛ in., and 40 mm for 1¼ in.). Clamp the front wheel tightly between your legs. Tighten the bearing cup by about ⅛ turn; then hold it tight with one wrench, while you tighten the locknut (see photo top left). Check and repeat as necessary until the bearing turns freely but is not loose.

ADJUSTING A THREADLESS HEADSET

All you need for this job is a 6 mm Allen wrench. First loosen the bolts that clamp the handlebar stem around the fork's steerer tube by one or two turns (see middle photo, above). Holding the handlebars with one hand, tighten the Allen bolt on top in stages of ¼ turn to tighten the headset (see right-hand photo, above). Tighten the stem clamp bolts again when the headset adjustment feels right.

QUICK CHECK

Here's a quick and easy way to make sure the headset is not too tight: Raise the front wheel off the ground by lifting it at the top tube. If you give the handlebars a little push, they should rotate sideways all the way without getting caught anywhere in between. Finally check for bearing play in accordance with the instruction "Bearing Check."

MAINTENANCE

If your headset is not equipped with enclosed machine bearings but with conventional open bearing rings, it should be overhauled at least once a year. Remove the handlebars with the stem; completely disassemble the headset; and remove the front fork, catching all bearing parts in a cloth.

Clean everything scrupulously and pack the bearing rings with grease; then embed the bearing rings in the grease. Reassemble in reverse sequence; finally install the handlebar with the stem, tightening it properly in the exact orientation lined up with the front wheel.

19 HANDLEBARS AND STEM

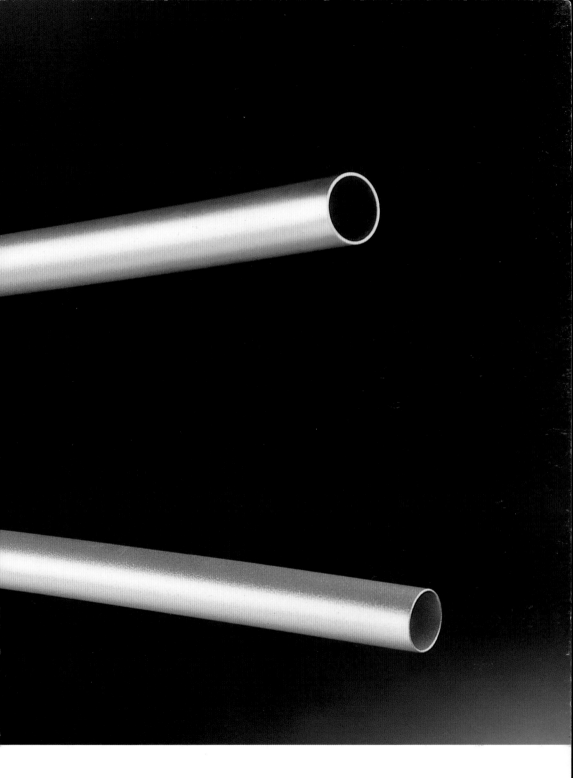

Together with the stem, the handlebars define the "cockpit" of your mountain bike. The way you select type and size is crucial to your riding position and comfort on the bike. In this chapter, you'll learn all there is to know about stems and handlebars.

Handlebar stems are available in even more diversity than handlebars themselves—steel, aluminum, or titanium, plain or colored, welded or cast, and all that in different lengths, diameters, and angles. Confusing? We'll help you along.

The most important criterion in the selection of a stem is that it must match the handlebars and the steerer tube. Preferably, they should both be made of the same material—both steel, both aluminum, or both titanium. To give an example, when clamping (relatively soft) aluminum handlebars in a (relatively hard) steel stem, you may damage the handlebars in such a way that it may break at the location where the two meet, which is due to the creation of a stress raiser, leading to fatigue failure—a catastrophic failure after extended use.

Even when using identical materials for stem and handlebars, the manufacturer may recommend you install a sleeve to spread the load around the point where the handlebars are clamped into the stem, which you should not neglect to do. Such sleeves are particularly necessary on titanium and carbon-fiber handlebars, which are often made out of very thin-walled materials and need the extra reinforcement sleeve to spread the load over a larger area.

Despite the recent introduction of items made of those "exotic" materials, aluminum alloy remains the material of choice for about 90 percent of the high-end mountain bikes sold, so there's little chance of getting a bad combination of materials if you buy a complete bike. But it is important to know which materials to use if you plan to assemble a bike to your own specifications or to replace the stem and/or handlebars.

The choice of stem configuration allows you to make rider position corrections: They come in different lengths, from 60 to 150 mm, and different rise angles, from 0 to 40 degrees.

Although still around, stems for use with threaded headsets are becoming a rarity in the world of mountain biking, corresponding with the sea change in headset design covered in the preceding chapter. Those stems of yore were installed inside the fork's steerer tube and held in place with a conical or wedge-shaped nut at the end of the correspondingly shaped stem. Nothing wrong with them, certainly if they're an oversize design (for 1¼ in. or 1⅛ in. diameter steerer tube), but they're getting rather thin on the ground

and you won't easily find suitable replacement parts.

The modern standard is based on compatibility with the threadless headset, and even within that category there are those same three different diameters, amongst which 1⅛ has become the virtual standard for all but special purpose bikes (while the 1 in. size is used mainly for road bikes, city bikes, and hybrids). The threadless headset itself is simpler and easier to adjust and install, and so is the stem that goes with it. Since it also eliminates the need

to cut screw thread on the fork stem, it's really no surprise that this system has become nearly universal. All you need do is cut the fork shaft to size, install

Lightweight amongst handlebars: 140 g carbon-fiber bars, that should not be installed without a protective sleeve between it and the stem clamp.

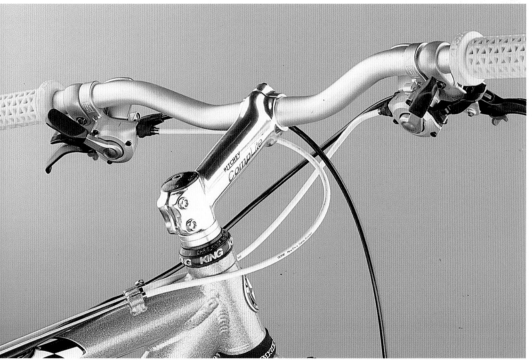

higher: If three or four spacers, adding up to 10 mm (⅜ in.), won't do it for you, you've got a frame that's too small. Using more space between the stem and the top of the headset will cause the headset to work itself loose over time, which will destroy it in short order.

Even though spacers aren't the way to go, there are other ways to

be mounted upside down for more or less rise.

To replace the stem, make sure the bike's front wheel is resting on solid ground. Remove the adjusting Allen bolt on top of the stem, as well as the plastic or aluminum cap under that bolt. Then undo both sets of Allen bolts on the stem (both the ones that clamp the stem around the steerer tube and those clamping in the han-

"Upswing" handlebars, as used originally for downhill and trials riding, are becoming more popular on standard mountain bikes. Their advantage is a more upright rider position (and you can make minor adjustments to the rider position by rotating them more or less).

whatever spacers are required to get up to the desired handlebar height (in combination with the stem's length and angle), and you're in business. We don't recommend using spacers indiscriminately to raise the handlebars

achieve a higher handlebar position: You can either get a stem with more "rise" (the vertical distance between the top of the headset and the center of the handlebars), or you can get a so-called flip-flop stem, which can

dlebars), and pull the stem off the steerer tube. Now you can replace the stem or turn it upside-down. Reinstall the stem loosely on the steerer tube; install the end cap and the adjusting bolt, tightening it only so far that the headset is

correctly adjusted, and then tighten the clamp bolts fully. Finally install the handlebars with the clamp in front, tightening the clamping bolts firmly.

Downhill handlebars had better be strong. This one is equipped with a clamped-on reinforcing brace, which can also be added to models that are supplied without.

Another advantage of the current style of stems with a separate clamp for the handlebars is that they make it easy to remove the handlebars for transportation or storage of the bike.

With respect to the dimensioning of the stem, the effects are:

▪ Longer stems with little rise retard steering motion, making the bike better for going straight than for quick cornering. The resulting rider position is stretched out, and not comfortable for most riders.

▪ Shorter stems with more rise lead to increased steering response and agility, while taking some of the load of the rider's back and shoulders.

Different stem lengths and rise rates can help adapt an otherwise poorly fitting frame to a rider, but that's really not to be done indiscriminately, because steering characteristics are also affected. Thus, using a long stem on a frame that's a little short for you may well result in a more comfortable riding position; but whether you appreciate the sluggish steering response that results is a different matter.

The kind of riders who are well served with a relatively short stem but a high position include downhill-riders, freeriders, and touring bikers, all of whom will want the better view over the terrain ahead of them. On the other hand, touring riders would benefit more from a smaller bike and a longer stem to keep the front end of the bike from being steered too easily. As in so many things, it's all a matter of compromises, and it'll be your task to find the compromise solutions that best suit your riding style.

For downhill use, there are special stubby stems (about 80 mm), resulting in a relatively upright riding position, even on a bike with a long top tube, which is common on that type of bike.

Modern aluminum stems have two bolts to clamp them vertically around the steerer tube and a separate clamp piece with another two bolts to hold in the handlebars.

In combination with the raised profile downhill handlebars, you get a pretty upright position.

Another often overlooked factor is the width of the handlebars. Early mountain bikes had enormously wide handlebars, and for many years the trend was to narrower models. However, in recent years there's

may be necessary for real downhill racing, it may be more than you'll need for most normal riding conditions (It will spread your arms quite far apart). You can safely take off about about 10 to 15 mm (⅜ in. to ⅝ in.) from both sides of such wide handlebars. Mark the correct location, measured from both ends first with a felt-tip pen before you start cutting into

Trendy bar: "Vario" handlebars and stem combination, which allows a choice of height and of handlebar-to seat distance. (Also note the markings for handlebar width, suggesting it's OK to cut them to size.)

been a reversal of this trend, and with the popularity of freeride and downhill bikes, manufacturers are once more making them in gorilla sizes. Yes, you can cut them down, but no, the manufacturers of bike and handlebars will probably void your warranty and deny any responsibility if you have an accident (as

the metal. Syntace makes a special tubing cutter for bicycle use, but you can also use the cheaper ones available in the hardware shop's plumbing section.

Of course, that applies to regular cross-country style mountain bikes. Downhill bikes often come with handlebars that are as wide as 700 to 800 mm, giving more control over the bike on steep drop-offs, and that's not the kind of condition for which to start cutting down on your handlebar's width. Ideally, you should try out any new or different handlebar configuration on a test bike (borrow one from an acquaintance if the bike store can't help you).

Usually bikes with frame sizes 46 to 50 cm (18 to 19½ in.) come equipped with a 130 mm long stem with 15 to 25 degrees of rise, and in recent years the trend has been toward shorter stems. If you're not comfortable, you will probably be able to find enough choice in stems that are shorter or longer, with more or less rise, or handlebars that sweep up (or down, if you prefer to reverse them) to adapt almost any bike that's average as it leaves the showroom floor to your special needs.

will the shop that sold you these items), so you'd better know what you're doing and do it right.

These days, the standard handlebar width is around 560 to 580 mm (22 in. to 22¾ in.). Although that

An optical treat: Beautifully welded and machined stem. An expensive way to make a stem, but probably not very light.

145

20 SEAT AND SEATPOST

If there's one thing that discourages biking, it's "saddle fear." Indeed, too many mountain bikers are uncomfortable due to a poor choice or adjustment of their seat. It may be the wrong shape or size or, more likely, it should be readjusted. Let's see what we can do about that.

Do bike seats cause impotence? No, they probably don't:The still frequently (mis-) quoted test that circulated in the general press as well as the cycling press some years ago, was based on a comparison of apples to oranges (the age category of male cyclists was much higher than that of the swimmers and runners tested). Just the same, there are obviously enough problems with most people's bike seats to justify an entire chapter devoted to the subject.

The seat is the interface between man and machine, and it's been whispered that more bicycle-related patents have been devoted to presumed enhancement of this vital interface than to all other bicycle components combined. Be that as it may, bike seats even today come in a variety of shapes and materials, and surely there should be one that's at least adequately comfortable for you. Very often, it's not so much the seat itself that's the culprit, but the way it's adjusted, so we'll be looking at that too, and the way it's adjusted is by means of the seatpost that holds it to the bike frame.

A recess or cutout in the central part of the seat is meant to relieve the friction at the point of greatest pressure.

Any bike seat is a compromise between a number of partly mutually exclusive criteria. Take the shape of the seat, for instance: A firm, long, narrow front portion is needed to provide the required freedom of movement combined with directional stability of the leg motion. That may be fine for the guy with quads of steel, but what about the rest of us? Isn't it asking a bit too much to expect us to sit on what seems like a steel rail? Then the thing gets wider toward the back, and your pelvic bones are supposed to find support there.

But off-road, you may have to slip off your seat either to the front or the back quickly and unobtrusively to save the day or just to transfer your weight back for a descent. So the mountain biker's seat should not be quite so pointed in the front and not quite so wide in the back.

And then consider the support the seat is supposed to provide to

SEAT ADJUSTMENTS

1. Before you make any other adjustments, use a level to align the top of the saddle perfectly horizontal.
2. You can achieve a more or less "stretched out" rider posture by sliding the seat further back or forward respectively. Work on it until you feel comfortable.
3. This is how you prevent develop knee problems: Place the cranks horizontally and use a plumb bob (a weight on a string) to make sure that the front of your knee cap is aligned vertically above the pedal spindle (center of the pedal) that is in front.
4. Seat height: When seated, you should be able to reach the lower pedal with the heel of your foot with the leg stretched.
5. If you experience numbness in the seat area, you can tilt the saddle so that the tip points down just a tad. This redistributes your weight so more of it rests on the rear of the seat.

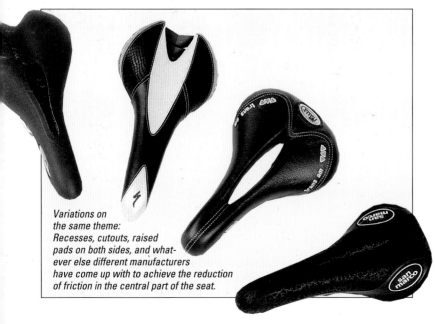

Variations on the same theme: Recesses, cutouts, raised pads on both sides, and whatever else different manufacturers have come up with to achieve the reduction of friction in the central part of the seat.

your pelvic bones (the reason seats are wider in the back). But are my pelvic bones in the same place as your's, and what about the difference between men and women? OK, so it's a matter of compromise, and all we can seriously suggest is that you look for a model that's got at least some of the features you cherish most.

Padding is one of the features often touted as being a feature of some seats to make them more comfortable, but even that's not necessarily so: The padding has to be thin and stiff enough for not hinder your movements on the one hand and your bones not to pierce through it on the other. However, in recent years, quite a number of manufacturers have taken up the gauntlet and designed such a wide range of shapes that something comfortable for mountain biking can be found amongst their products.

Many of today's generation of seats have a recess or even a gap in the center section of the top. These are intended to move some of the pressure away from the connective tissues between the legs, which is not suitable for carrying the load of a seated cyclist. Combining this general shape with various narrower or wider, more or less firmly padded sections in the back, and more or less springiness in the overall structure has done a lot to improve comfort for many mountain bikers, and you may be amongst them.

Some seats are built for minimum weight, and although we love our bits of titanium as much as the next bicycle fanatic, it hardly seems to be an important criterion until you've established a shape that you find comfortable. The second materials issue is whether or not to use a form-fitting gel material inside. Trickled down from the wheelchair industry is a gel material that conforms to the rider's shape, but on the bike that shape is always changing due to movement, and consequelty even this presumed wonder material isn't fulfilling its promise in our book. And finally, on the subject of materials, should the cover be made of plastic, nylon, smooth or rough leather, or something else?

In general, most riders find a soft, thin leather cover (preferably rough in the middle section but smooth on the sides) most comfortable, although Kevlar seems to be as comfortable and is certainly more durable. On the other hand,

Selle Italia's Flite model is considered the most comfortable conventional saddle on the market for male mountain bikers.

Kevlar is not quite as immune to dirt and moisture as treated leather, and that's the reason why some manufacturers use Kevlar only on the corners where leather might get damaged more easily.

Downhillers and freestyle riders need even more freedom of movement in (and around) their seats than the average mountain biker, and anyone riding a full-suspension bike will have to transfer his or her weight forward frequently to put more of the weight over the front wheel and to compensate for the amount of suspension travel. Specific downhill seat models allow more of this kind of

movement while still staying seated due to their greater length, and they tend to have a slightly more voluminous and better padded front portion. Some other riders may find this to be advantageous as well, since it takes the pressure off the sensitive area. But real cross-country riders are skeptical about that much length, thickness, and padding, which add more weight than needed as well.

One of the most successful seat designs is that of Sella Italia's Flite model. It has a somewhat flexible shell that's suspended between firm ends at the front and the back. Shaped well and with very little padding needed to cover up bad basic design, they are many riders' first choice. And this is one design that does benefit from titanium construction for the wires that hold it all together, because it provides just enough springiness without being "spongy."

Of special concern in recent years (apart from the "impotence hoax" mentioned in the opening paragraph, which obviously applied to men only) has been the comfort of bike seats for women.

SEAT SELECTION TIPS

- The only way to be sure a particular type of saddle is comfortable for a specific user is by means of an extended test ride.

- Try to find a bike shop where they'll actually agree to let you test ride a seat for a weekend before you buy. Or perhaps you can make some kind of favorable exchange arrangement.

- Check to make sure the seat can easily be mounted to the seatpost you have selected (or vice versa).

- Good looks and comfort are not necessarily synonymous when it comes to mountain bike seats, although they're certainly not mutually exclusive either. The pretty narrow seats may look elegant, but they may be unsuitable for the somewhat upright riding posture typical for most mountain biking situations.

Indeed, many seat manufacturers have brought out special women's versions of their seats, which usually means wider in the back, shorter in the front, and more padding especially in the front area. However, it's been established reasonably well that what matters most for most women's comfort (apart from a wider back, which is anatomically justified) is a recessed section in the middle portion of the seat, and indeed such models are now widely available.

Probably more important than any other feature on the mountain bike seat is the question about how well it can be adjusted. If you can't accurately move the seat forward or back, up or down, tilting more or less in controlled intervals, you're apt to loose any advantages that you had hoped to obtain from that optimum design you selected. Part of the adjustability depends on the seatpost, but some of it is inherent in the seat's

own features. Basically, the seat's wires (whether steel or titanium) should be exact-

This lightweight aluminum seatpost has a seat adjusting mechanism that's offset to the rear more than it is on most other models, making it possible to increase the distance from the handlebars.

Shown upside down: Suspension seatposts, like this one from Rock Shox, add comfort; but they don't offer the equivalent of a rear suspension.

ly parallel at the right distance corresponding to the width of the seatpost's clamp over the longest possible distance, and there should be enough space between the top of those wires and the saddle cover for the adjustable clamp to fit without coming into contact with the saddle cover.

ALL ABOUT SEATPOSTS

Simple though it seams, the seatpost is actually a very sensitive, and often troublesome, component on the mountain bike. Firstly, it has to be long enough for the seat to be placed high enough above the pedals, still allowing at least 65 mm (2½ in) to be clamped in the seat tube. Any less, and you risk it coming out, e.g. in a jump or when you suddenly land on the seat unintentionally.

Then it has to be the right outside diameter to fit inside the seat tube, and the availability of seatposts ranging in diameter between 26.8 and 31.8 mm means there's a serious risk of grabbing

one that doesn't fit properly. When buying a new one, take the bike to the shop and have the sales clerk measure and fit it for you, rather than risk scratching one up in your own attempt to establish whether you picked the right size.

To adjust the height of the seat, or to install or remove a seatpost, mountain bikes traditionally use a quick-release binder bolt, which works just like the one on the wheel hubs. Since only fast downhills really call for seat height changes from the comfortable standard height, several manufacturers have abandoned that device in favor of the cheaper, and lighter, Allen-type binder bolt used on road bikes.

If a seatpost gets stuck inside the seat tube and won't be budged, whatever you do, leave the seat installed on it. You'll want to use its leverage to help twist and pull the seatpost out (if stuck, first try to remove it, even if you actually wanted to lower it, lest it gets stuck even more solidly). If still no luck, remove the binder bolt all the way and pour some penetrating oil in at the slotted top of the seat tube, leaving it to stand for 5 minutes or so before trying again. If it was an oversized seatpost, replace it with one of the correct size, but if rust and dirt were the cause, use wire wool on the outside of the post and sandpaper wrapped around e.g. a long stick or screwdriver to clean up the inside of the seat tube. Then apply a generous dab of grease to the inside of the tube or the outside of the post and install it at the desired height, clamping it down hard with the binder bolt.

The clip on top of the seatpost is used for the adjustments involving the longitudinal position relative to the center of the seatpost and the angle of the seat relative to the horizontal plane. Some of the most expensive seatposts on the market have separate adjustment bolts for the adjustment of the longitudinal position and the angle. As pointed out before, many mountain bike seatposts can actually be reversed to increase the distance between the handlebars and the seat.

Moving the seat back or forth by half an inch or so can make a big change in the amount by which you have to stretch out to reach the handlebars without replacing the stem. Bigger changes may negatively affect your balance on the bike, so we suggest you experiment with changing the position in small steps of perhaps ¼ in. at a time and consider a longer

Finally a few words about suspension seatposts. They're a simple way of adding suspension to a hardtail bike, but not a safe addition to a full-suspension bike: The two suspension methods will work against each other, and you may lose control of the bike and destroy the suspension. The best models are well damped, so you won't find yourself constantly moving up and down while pedaling. Even so, it's a matter of personal preference, and an acceptable way of making a hardtail just a little softer without breaking the bank.

This sophisticated seatpost has separate and accurate adjustment mechanisms for the seat angle and the seat's longitudinal position.

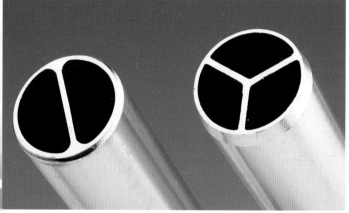

If you're a heavy rider, or if you take your mountain bike for sercious jumps, an internally reinforced seatpost like these are a worthwhile investment.

A simple, and not fine-tuneable seatpost. It is operated by a single bolt for clamping, and can be held in place with a little grub screw.

or shorter stem if you can't make yourself comfortable by changing the saddle position. Changing the angle of tilt of the top of the seat can bring a significant improvement in the comfort on the seat, so it's worthwhile experimenting with this adjustment before spending money on a different seat, which may turn out to be no more comfortable. In general, men tend to tilt the nose up a little relative to the horizontal plane, while most women tilt it down a little. But you may find it more comfortable to deviate from that general rule.

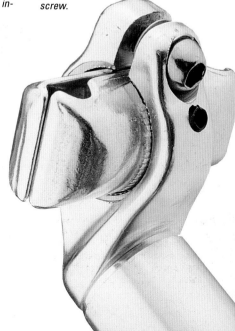

INDEX